THE GODDESS GATEWAY

Copyright © 2026 by Dr. Camille Valentine

All rights reserved. No part of this book may be reproduced in any manner whatsoever without written permission except in the case of brief quotations embodied in critical articles and reviews.

First Printing, 2026

The Goddess Gateway

Dr. Camille Valentine

Contents

Dedication		vii
1	The Remembering Calls You Home	1
2	Breaking the Ancestral Silence Contract	8
3	The Alchemy of Integration	12
4	The Sacred Art of Divine Boundaries	26
5	Alchemy of the Wounded Healer	33
6	Reclaiming Your Throne Room Voice	41
7	The Mirror Work of Authentic Authority	48
8	Dancing with Resistance and Revelation	57
9	Building Your Sacred Constellation	68
10	Designing Your Liberation Legacy	79
11	Wealth as Spiritual Practice and Social Justice	91
12	Crowning the Sovereign Queen Within	106
13	APPENDIX A	118
About the Author		124
Acknowledgements		126

The Goddess Gateway

A Leadership Journey to Sovereign Power

Dr. Camille Valentine

To my mother, Marilyn Kellum

who taught me unconditional love

and that beauty, style, and grace can coexist in the same woman, fully, effortlessly, and unapologetically. Rest in Power.

To my Aunt Kimberly Kellum,

whose wisdom, steadiness, and fierce devotion have carried me through every season of becoming.

And to every professional woman of color

compressed by the weight of oppression,

broken by systems that sought to silence you, abused by environments that demanded more than they ever gave,

yet awakened now to your own North Star...

This book is for you....

For the woman who rises again,

and again,

and again.

May these pages be your gateway back to your sovereign

1

The Remembering Calls You Home

Your soul has been sending distress signals.

Those 3 AM wake-ups when your purpose pounds against your ribs like a caged bird? That's not insomnia—that's your inner divinity refusing to let you sleep through your own life.

The mysterious illnesses that force rest, making you lie down when you won't slow down? Your body staging interventions your mind won't allow.

The recurring dreams where you're running, flying, breaking free? Your soul is drawing maps to territories you've abandoned.

Feel it? The knowing that rises when you read these words? That's not imagination—that's recognition. The symptoms aren't signs of your failure but of your awakening:

The impostor syndrome that haunts you despite degrees and accolades? It's not personal inadequacy—it's your soul's allergic reaction to performing a pale version of your power.

The tears that ambush you in the car between meetings? Not weakness—that's grief for the parts of yourself you've had to bury to be taken seriously.

The drain that follows "successful" presentations? Not introversion—that's the exhaustion of channeling your brilliance through filters that dilute its frequency.

The synchronicities you're too scared to acknowledge? Not a coincidence—that's the universe desperately trying to remind you of who you really are.

These aren't distress signals—they're love letters from your soul, written in the ink of urgency, sealed with the wax of "How much longer will you pretend to be satisfied with crumbs when you were born for the feast?"

The cost of living in spiritual exile compounds like interest on a debt you never agreed to carry. Calculate it: The energy expenditure of maintaining separate personas—professional you, spiritual you, cultural you—as if you were three different women sharing one exhausted body.

The opportunities missed because you silenced intuition that could have saved you from bad deals, toxic partnerships, and paths that looked successful but felt like death.

The relationships that remain surface because you can't risk being seen, not when being seen has always meant being too much, too spiritual, too Black, too woman, too powerful for the rooms you've learned to shrink yourself to fit.

Patricia knows this cost. At 65, after 40 years of climbing ladders that leaned against the wrong buildings, she sits in her retirement with regrets that have nothing to do with career metrics.

"I spent four decades proving I belonged in rooms that were never going to see me as whole," she tells me, her voice carrying the weight of too much wisdom earned too late. "I wish I'd spent even half that energy building rooms where I could breathe."

And what of our daughters? Our spiritual daughters? Every time we fragment ourselves, we teach them that wholeness is a luxury they can't afford. Every time we silence our spiritual intelligence, we tell them our intuition is less valuable than intellect.

We become unwitting accomplices in our own oppression, passing down patterns of fragmentation like inherited China—precious but too delicate for daily use.

The organizations that miss out on our integrated wisdom? They're building strategies on half-truths, making decisions without the intelligence that comes from those who see beyond spreadsheets into spirit.

They're leaving money on the table because they can't access the innovation that comes from intuitive leaps. They're creating cultures of exhaustion because they've made no room for the sacred.

You've been trying to grow in a pot too small for your roots. You can survive—you have been surviving—but you'll never bloom into the fullness of what you came here to be.

But what if?

What if I told you there's another way? What if the exhaustion that brought you to this page was not evidence of your failure but of your readiness? What if everything you've been taught about having to choose between spirituality and success was a lie designed to keep you playing small?

Imagine walking into tomorrow's board meeting with your full power intact. Not aggressive. Not performing. Not code-switching until your tongue forgets its mother language. But sovereign. Centered.

Speaking from a place where strategy and spirit dance together like lovers who've never been separated. Imagine making decisions from the marriage of data and divinity, leading with metrics and magic, building success that feeds your soul instead of starving it.

The integration you seek isn't about being 'woo woo' at work, it's about accessing your complete intelligence. It's about recognizing that the voice telling you you're not ready is the same voice that knows exactly how ready you are—it's just been hired by your comfort zone to keep you safe from your own greatness.

This is what becomes available when you stop fragmenting yourself:

Dr. Amara Johnson, CEO of a healthcare conglomerate, now opens strategic planning sessions with grounding practices. Not because she's pushing spirituality on anyone, but because centered humans make better decisions.

Her company's innovation metrics increased by 45% in the first year of integration.

Investment banker turned conscious wealth advisor Folasade Williams follows her intuitive hits when analyzing portfolios. She calls it "pattern recognition beyond the obvious." Her clients call it the reason they trust her with generational wealth building.

Attorney Nia Baptiste stopped suppressing the energy readings she gets from every contract, every negotiation, every client. Now she prevents problems before they manifest, saving millions in litigation.

She doesn't call it prophecy in the courtroom. She calls it "comprehensive risk assessment."

These women aren't special. They're not more spiritual or more successful than you. They simply decided that the cost of fragmentation had become higher than the risk of integration. They chose wholeness, and wholeness chose them back.

Your throne awaits. Your ancestors are calling. Your future self is beckoning. Will you answer?

The first step through the gateway isn't a leap—it's a lean. A gentle leaning toward the truth of who you are when no one's watching, when the performance ends, when you finally stop auditioning for your own life and start living it.

Take out a piece of paper. Right now. Not tomorrow when you have time. Not next week when things calm down. Now, while the recognition is still warm in your chest, while your soul is still whispering "finally, finally, finally."

Write down three ways you've been fragmenting yourself. Be specific:
  "I hide my meditation practice from my team."
  "I silence my intuitive insights in strategy meetings."
  "I pretend I don't see energy dynamics in negotiations."

Now write three small ways you can begin integration this week. Small. Gentle. Doable:
  "I'll place my grandmother's ring on my desk as a sacred anchor."
  "I'll take three breaths before each meeting to connect with my intuition."
  "I'll speak one previously silenced truth in a safe professional context."

These aren't just action items. They're divine breadcrumbs leading you home to yourself. Each small integration creates an energetic shift that makes the next one easier. Each moment of wholeness weakens the walls between who you are and who you pretend to be.

Now stand. Place one hand on your heart and one hand on your crown. Feel the connection between your human self and your divine nature. Speak these words aloud—yes, aloud, even if it feels uncomfortable, especially if it feels uncomfortable:

"I am a sovereign leader whose spiritual wisdom enhances my professional power. I release all contracts that require me to fragment myself for false safety.

I choose wholeness. I choose integration. I choose to lead with the full spectrum of my divine intelligence. And so it is."

Feel that shift? That subtle but unmistakable loosening in your chest? That's not just hope—that's your energy reorganizing itself around a new commitment.

That's your soul recognizing that the exile is ending. That's your ancestors celebrating that their sacrifices weren't in vain, that you're about to alchemize their struggles into your sovereignty.

This is only the beginning. Each chapter ahead offers another piece of your sovereignty puzzle, another key to rooms within yourself you've kept locked.

Chapter by chapter, you'll reclaim what was always yours: the divine feminine leadership that flows through your bloodline like rivers of liquid gold, waiting to nourish everything you touch.

The corner office can have life. The boardroom can hold the sacred. Success can feed your soul. But first, you must remember who you are beneath the titles, beyond the performance, before the world told you that power required pretense.

Your remembering calls you home. Will you answer?

2

Breaking the Ancestral Silence Contract

Let's map your maternal lineage of silence.

Take a moment. Breathe into the knowing that's about to surface. Ask yourself:

What gifts did your grandmother or great-grandmother hide? Perhaps she saw spirits but called them intuition. Maybe she healed with touch, but only in her kitchen, only with family, only when no one important was watching. She might have prophesied in dreams but shared them as concerns, watering down divine intelligence until it was weak enough to swallow.

How did your mother code-switch? Watch the memory of her voice—how it changed between home and work, between family and white folks, between her truth and their comfort. Notice how she taught you without words that there were parts of yourself too dangerous for display, parts that needed to stay home like good china, saved for special occasions that never came.

What spiritual practices were abandoned for "respectability"? The altar that became a "decorative table." The crystals rebranded as "pretty rocks." The sage burning transformed into "air freshener." The prayers that shifted from embodied ritual to silent, still politeness.

You're not alone in this archaeological dig. Across professions, across generations, the patterns repeat:

The healer who became a nurse but never speaks of the energy she feels pulsing between her hands and her patients' pain

The prophet who channeled her visions into "strategic planning," never admitting she sees the future in meditation before she maps it in spreadsheets

The priestess who hid her altar when company came, who learned to pray in silence so deep even God had to strain to hear

These women aren't weak. They're brilliant strategists who understood the mathematics of survival in a world that burned witches, pathologized prophets, and institutionalized anyone too magical for comfort. They signed silence contracts because the alternative was erasure—literal, violent, complete.

The historical record writes itself in blood and silence. During slavery, our spiritual practices were outlawed because our oppressors understood something we've been trained to forget: spiritual power is real power. They knew that a people connected to divine source, to ancestral wisdom, to the intelligence of the universe itself, could never be truly enslaved. So they made our drums illegal, our gatherings suspicious, our healing criminal.

Jim Crow dressed the violence in respectability politics. Suddenly, it wasn't enough to survive—you had to prove you deserved to survive by being exceptional. But exceptional within their definitions. Exceptional without the mess of spirituality, the wildness of intuition, the danger of women who knew things without being taught by their institutions.

Integration demanded a different sacrifice: assimilate or stay outside. Bring your body, but leave your soul at the door. Contribute your labor but not your knowing. Be diverse in appearance but uniform in expression. The silence contract updated its terms but never released its signatories.

The contract your grandmother signed in 1943 is still being auto-renewed in your 2026 consciousness, charging interest you can't afford to pay.

Epigenetics researchers discovered something that changes everything: trauma doesn't just live in our memories—it imprints itself onto our DNA like a biological contract. It is as if the body has signed an agreement with pain, silently passing the terms down from one generation to the next. This is why we sometimes feel that tightness in our neck before we try to speak our truth.

Why do our palms sweat when a shadow from the past hovers too close? Why do our knees weaken when a trigger pushes us back into an old, familiar wound that should have been healed long ago? These responses are not random. They are written into us, coded into the very instructions of our being. Epigenetics shows us that trauma is not simply a personal burden but a cellular inheritance.

The body remembers what the mind tries to forget. And if we do not heal, trauma doesn't just remain in the psyche—it becomes trapped in our muscles, our breath, our blood.

Over time, that trapped energy begins to fester. It calcifies into patterns, rewrites our immune responses, and compromises our vitality. Left unresolved, it evolves into disease—chronic pain, autoimmune disorders, hypertension, even cancers. The body's "biological contract" with trauma can transform into a death sentence if it is not renegotiated. But here is the truth that offers us power: contracts can be broken. Epigenetic changes are not permanent.

Healing work—whether through therapy, breathwork, ritual, ancestral repair, or embodied practices—literally has the ability to rewrite our cellular story. We can interrupt the cycle and free not just ourselves, but future generations from the weight of pain we never agreed to carry.

When we release trauma, we reclaim the body's original agreement with life: to be whole, sovereign, and alive in our fullest power. Healing, then, is not just personal—it is ancestral, communal, and revolutionary.

3

The Alchemy of Integration

The Goddess Gateway Framework emerged not from theory but from necessity.

It was 3 AM on a Tuesday when the framework first revealed itself—that liminal hour when the veil between worlds is thinnest, when ancestors speak clearest, when truth refuses to be dressed in acceptable clothing. She'd been lying awake, feeling the familiar split between who she was and who she had to be, when suddenly she saw it: four doorways appearing in her mind's eye, each one offering passage from fragmentation to wholeness.

The framework that would become her liberation—and now yours—has four pillars, each one a doorway to pass through on your journey from exhausted performance to embodied power.

Recognition: The first doorway requires you to see clearly what is. Not the story you tell yourself about "having it all together" or "making it work," but the raw truth of your fragmentation. This is where you map the geography of your splitting—identifying exactly where and how you fracture yourself for acceptance, for safety, for success that tastes like sawdust.

Recognition sounds like: "I modulate my voice seventeen times a day. I hide my altar before video calls. I translate my knowing into their language until I forget my mother tongue. I am succeeding at being who they need me to be and failing at being who I am."

Recognition feels like: Relief mixed with grief. Relief that you're finally telling the truth. Grief for how long you've been living the lie.

Reclamation: The second doorway invites you to gather your scattered pieces—not to glue them back together like a broken vase, but to honor each fragment as sacred. Every piece of you that you've hidden contains medicine. Your spiritual wisdom isn't separate from your strategic brilliance—they're dance partners who've been forced to perform solo.

Reclamation looks like: Making a list of every part of yourself you've hidden or minimized. Your intuitive knowing. Your ancestor reverence. Your emotional intelligence. Your body wisdom. Your cultural expressions. Your spiritual practices.

Then asking: What gift does each piece carry? What power have I been denying myself and my work?

Reclamation feels like: Coming home to rooms in yourself you'd forgotten existed. Like finding treasures you'd buried for safekeeping and realizing you're finally safe enough to wear them.

Integration: The third doorway is where alchemy happens. This isn't about balance—that exhausting myth that keeps you juggling. This is about fusion. Like a master alchemist, you're taking the base metals of your separate selves and transmuting them into gold. Your spiritual wisdom infuses your strategic planning. Your ancestral knowing informs your leadership decisions. Your intuition and analysis dance together in boardrooms.

Integration looks like: Opening a strategic planning session with thirty seconds of centering breath. Presenting intuitive insights as "pattern recognition based on deep analysis." Wearing your great-grandmother's ring to board meetings as a reminder of whose shoulders you stand on. Speaking in your full voice—the one that carries your ancestors' wisdom and your professional expertise in the same breath.

Integration feels like: The relief of taking off a too-tight shoe. The expansion in your chest when you stop holding your breath. The click of puzzle pieces finally fitting together.

Embodiment: The fourth doorway transforms integration from concept to lived reality. This is where you stop practicing wholeness and start being it. Your integrated self becomes so natural that fragmentation feels foreign. You lead from a place where spiritual and strategic are not two but one, where your power comes not from perfecting performance but from embodying presence.

Embodiment looks like: Walking into rooms with the full weight of your wisdom. Making decisions from the marriage of intuition and analysis. Creating innovations that honor both profit and purpose. Leading teams with the perfect blend of compassion and clarity. Being the same person in the boardroom and at your altar—not because you're performing spirituality at work or bringing corporate energy to sacred space, but because you've transcended the false division.

Embodiment feels like: Sovereignty. Like wearing a crown that was always yours but you'd been told was too heavy, too much, too threatening. It feels like power that doesn't deplete but regenerates. Like being a diamond—multifaceted but undivided, each face reflecting the same light differently.

This isn't about balance. Balance keeps you juggling, struggling, managing the impossible task of keeping all balls in the air. This is about fusion—creating something new from the marriage of all you are. Imagine trying to balance hydrogen and oxygen. Exhausting. Impossible. But fuse them? You get water—something essential, powerful, flowing.

You are not meant to balance your spiritual and professional selves. You're meant to fuse them into something the world has never seen but desperately needs: integrated sovereign leadership that transforms everything it touches.

Neuroscience tells us what our bodies already know: fragmentation literally splits our neural networks.

When you code-switch, your brain creates competing command centers, each one requiring energy to maintain, each one fighting for dominance. The cognitive load is equivalent to running multiple operating systems simultaneously—no wonder you're exhausted before lunch. No wonder Sunday night fills you with dread. No wonder you need a vacation from your vacation, because even rest requires deciding which self gets to relax.

Dr. Keisha Mack's research on code-switching in professional Black women found cortisol levels—the stress hormone—spike an average of 40% during voice modulation alone. Think about that. Just changing how you speak floods your body with the same stress hormones released when facing physical danger. Your body reads fragmentation as a threat because it is—it's a threat to your integrated wholeness, your divine design, your sovereign nature.

But here's what changes everything: the same research shows that when Black women lead from integrated authenticity, their cortisol levels don't just normalize—they drop below baseline. Integration isn't just less stressful than fragmentation; it's actively restorative. Your body rewards wholeness with the neurochemicals of thriving: increased oxytocin (connection), elevated dopamine (satisfaction), enhanced serotonin (well-being).

The science confirms what our ancestors knew without needing studies: wholeness is our natural state. Fragmentation is the imposed condition.

Consider the concept of àṣẹ from Yoruba tradition—the power to make things happen, the life force that flows through all things. Àṣẹ doesn't fragment. It doesn't split itself to be acceptable. It flows whole and undivided, creating change through its unified presence. Your ancestors didn't separate sacred from secular, spiritual from strategic. The medicine woman was also the strategic advisor. The priestess was also a political force. The griot was both a spiritual keeper and a practical historian.

This ancient wisdom finds echo in modern quantum physics. Coherence—when all waves align in phase—creates exponentially more power than scattered frequencies. When you integrate, you stop canceling out your own power through interference patterns. You become coherent. You become powerful. You become unstoppable.

The false split between spiritual and professional wasn't created by you—it was imposed upon you by systems that profit from your diminishment. The corporate world that says "leave your whole self at the door" fears your wholeness because integrated beings can't be controlled, can't be gaslit, can't be convinced that exploitation is opportunity.

When you integrate, you don't just heal yourself—you become ungovernable by systems that require your fragmentation.

Let me show you what integration looks like in the boardroom, in the strategy session, in the moment-to-moment navigation of leadership.

Aisha discovered integration not through theory but through exhaustion-driven experimentation. As CFO of a healthcare technology company, she'd spent three years perfecting the performance of "data-driven leader" while her intuitive knowing—the same knowing that had guided her to every major breakthrough—remained locked away like a guilty secret.

The shift began small. Before her weekly finance meetings, she started taking thirty seconds in the bathroom to center herself—hand on heart, three deep breaths, a whispered "Guide me to highest good for all." She didn't announce this practice. She simply arrived differently. Her team noticed immediately. "You seem more present," they said. "More grounded."

Encouraged, she began translating her spiritual insights into strategic language. When her morning meditation revealed concerns about a potential acquisition—the energy felt scattered, unaligned—she presented it as "identifying cultural integration risks that could impact ROI." When her body wisdom signaled that a vendor was untrustworthy—that tightening in her solar plexus she'd learned to read like a Bloomberg terminal—she framed it as "risk indicators requiring deeper due diligence."

The revelation came during a product development meeting. The team was stuck, cycling through the same stale ideas. The ancestors whispered: "Empty the vessel." Without overthinking, Aisha suggested a two-minute silent reflection. "Let's just breathe and see what emerges." She could feel the resistance, the eye rolls barely suppressed. But she held steady in her knowing.

Two minutes of silence. Then the junior developer—usually silent in these meetings—shared an innovative approach that would eventually become their flagship feature. "I don't know where that came from," he said. Aisha did. She'd created space for wisdom to enter.

Within six months, her integrated approach had transformed not just her leadership but her entire division. Meeting productivity increased 35%—not because she'd implemented a new framework but because she'd created space for whole humans to show up. Innovation metrics soared because intuition was given an equal seat at the table with analysis. Team retention hit 94% because people finally felt seen in their fullness.

But here's the key: she never once used the words "spiritual" or "intuitive" in her professional communications. She learned the art of translation:

"Let's take a moment to center" instead of "Let's ground our energy."

"I'm sensing some resistance to this direction," instead of "The energy feels blocked."

"My experience suggests we pause here," instead of "My guides are saying wait."

"What's your body telling you about this decision?" instead of "What's your intuitive hit?"

This isn't hiding—it's strategic revelation. You're not dimming your light; you're adjusting the frequency so it can be received.

Marcus, her colleague in engineering, provides another model. As a senior director who practices Ifá, he'd hidden his spiritual practice for a decade, exhausted by the split between his morning divination practice and his afternoon engineering reviews. His integration began with a simple shift: viewing his code reviews as a form of divination—reading patterns, identifying what's hidden, predicting future states from present signs.

He started incorporating principles from Ifá into his project management without naming them as such. The concept of èbó (sacrifice) became "strategic resource allocation for maximum impact." The practice of consulting the oracle became "systematic pattern analysis for decision-making." The understanding of àṣẹ (life force) became "optimizing team energy dynamics for peak performance."

His teams didn't know they were operating according to ancient African wisdom principles. They only knew that projects ran more smoothly, conflicts were resolved faster, and innovations emerged more frequently. Marcus had discovered the secret: integration doesn't require announcement—it requires embodiment.

The resistance will come. Count on it. Plan for it. Dance with it.

Internal resistance arrives first, dressed in the familiar clothing of your oldest fears. "Who do you think you are?" it whispers as you prepare to speak your integrated truth. "They'll think you've lost your mind," it warns as you bring wholeness to spaces that have only known your fragments.

This voice isn't your enemy—it's your protector, outdated but well-meaning, still running the ancient program that says visibility equals danger. Thank it for its service. Then update the software: "Thank you for protecting me when hiding was necessary for survival. We're safe to be seen now. Watch me create new possibilities."

Impostor syndrome will flare like a fever when you first integrate. Not because you're doing something wrong, but because you're doing something revolutionary. You're refusing to perform the acceptable version of yourself. You're showing up whole in spaces designed for fragments. Of course, the old programming resists—it's being overwritten.

Dr. Camille navigated this by creating what she called her "Integration Incubator, starting with the safest spaces first. She brought her integrated self to her therapist, her sister circle, and her meditation group. She practiced speaking in her full voice, sharing her whole knowing, being all of herself in these containers of safety. Each practice session built her integration muscle, preparing her for higher-stakes revelation.

External resistance has its own choreography. Organizations that profit from your fragmentation will push back against your wholeness. Colleagues comfortable with your diminished performance will bristle at your embodied power. Systems designed for controllable parts will malfunction when encountering an integrated whole.

Sarah's story illustrates the navigation. As she began integrating her indigenous wisdom practices with her leadership style, her supervisor grew increasingly uncomfortable. "You've changed" became the refrain. "You're less of a team player" meant she was no longer sacrificing herself on the altar of others' comfort.

She navigated with strategic brilliance:

Documenting every improvement in her team's metrics

Building alliances with other integrated leaders

Translating her transformation into bottom-line results

Maintaining impeccable professionalism while refusing to fragment

When the resistance peaked—a meeting where she was told her "new approach" was "concerning"—she responded with data. Increased innovation scores. Improved team engagement. Higher client satisfaction. "If my integration is concerning," she said calmly, "then perhaps we need to examine what we're actually optimizing for."

The room shifted. The resistance revealed itself as fear—fear of change, fear of power they couldn't control, fear of what her wholeness meant for their fragmentation.

Here's your resistance navigation toolkit:

For internal resistance:

Morning integration practice: five minutes visualizing yourself whole in challenging spaces

Somatic support: notice where resistance lives in your body, breathe into it

Evidence journal: document every positive outcome from integration

Anchor phrases: "My wholeness serves everyone," "Integration is my birthright."

For external resistance:

Strategic revelation: choose when and how much to reveal

Alliance building: find others hungry for integration

Results focus: let outcomes speak louder than explanations

Energy protection: visualize golden light protecting your integrated field

Remember: resistance is feedback. It tells you where the system is rigid, where change is needed, and where your medicine is most powerful. Don't fight it—alchemize it.

When you integrate, you become a tuning fork for wholeness.

Your coherent frequency creates resonance in others, awakening their own hunger for integration. This isn't metaphorical—it's physics. When a tuning fork vibrates at its natural frequency, other tuning forks in proximity begin vibrating at the same frequency. When you embody integrated leadership, you give others permission to seek their own wholeness.

The ripples begin immediately. Your assistant stops apologizing for her meditation practice. Your colleague brings his whole creative self to brainstorming sessions. Your direct report starts speaking in her natural voice, three octaves lower and infinitely more powerful than her "professional" voice.

Keandra watched this ripple effect transform her entire organization. As Chief Innovation Officer, she'd made a commitment to lead from integration—bringing her design thinking expertise AND her ancestral pattern recognition, her MBA training AND her body wisdom, her strategic acumen AND her spiritual insight.

The first ripple: her immediate team began experimenting with integration. The data analyst who also practiced numerology began finding patterns others missed. The project manager who studied indigenous time concepts revolutionized their scheduling approach. The UX designer who understood energy flow created interfaces that felt intuitively alive.

The second ripple: other departments took notice. "What's happening in Innovation?" became the water cooler question. Their projects were delivering faster, their solutions more elegant, and their team more engaged. Leaders started requesting transfers into Keandra's division—not for the projects but for the permission to be whole.

The third ripple: organizational transformation. Within eighteen months, the company had restructured its entire approach to leadership development, incorporating what they called "Whole Leader Principles"—really just integration by another name. Meeting structures changed. Performance metrics evolved. The culture shifted from exhausted fragmentation to energized coherence.

But here's what Keandra will tell you: she never set out to transform the organization. She simply committed to transforming herself, to refusing the daily fractioning, to showing up whole regardless of reception. The ripples were inevitable.

This is the science of energetic coherence. When you achieve internal integration, you create a coherent electromagnetic field that influences other fields around you. The HeartMath Institute has documented this: coherent heart rhythms in one person can entrain the heart rhythms of others in proximity. Your integration literally helps others integrate. Your wholeness calls forth their wholeness.

The implications are staggering. Every meeting you enter with integrated presence shifts the field. Every conversation held from wholeness creates possibility for others' wholeness. Every decision made from the marriage of spiritual and strategic sends ripples through the organizational matrix.

You're not just changing yourself—you're changing the template.

Your integration initiation awaits.

Gather three objects: something representing your spiritual self (perhaps a crystal, a prayer bead, a feather), something representing your professional self (a business card, a pen, a piece of your work), and something representing your integrated future (choose intuitively—trust what calls).

Sit quietly with these objects. Hold the spiritual object in your left hand, feeling its weight, its texture, its energy. This is the part of you that knows without thinking, that connects to mysteries beyond spreadsheets, that carries your ancestors' whispers and your soul's truth. Honor it. Thank it for surviving in hiding. Tell it: "You are welcome here. All of you."

Hold the professional object in your right hand. Feel its different energy—perhaps more structured, more boundaried, more externally focused. This is the part of you that navigates systems, that creates in the material world, that transforms vision into form. Honor it. Thank it for its service. Tell it: "You are not separate from my sacred self. You are sacred work in action."

Now bring your hands together, objects touching at the center of your chest. Feel them merge—not disappearing into each other but creating something new. An alloy. A fusion. A marriage.

Hold the third object—your integrated future. Let visions arise: You, walking into tomorrow's board meeting carrying all your wisdom. You, speaking in your full voice, feeling your ancestors nod in approval. You, making decisions from the sweet spot where intuition and analysis kiss. You, creating innovations that honor both profit and purpose, both heaven and earth.

Breathe into this vision. Let it sink into your bones, reprogram your cells, rewrite your neural pathways. You are not learning integration—you are remembering it. You are not becoming whole—you are revealing the wholeness that fragmentation could never actually break.

Take your journal. Write your Integration Intention: "This week, I will integrate by..."

Choose something specific. Perhaps: "I will begin each meeting with three centering breaths." Or: "I will speak one intuitive insight using strategic language." Or: "I will wear my grandmother's ring to remind me I'm never alone in that boardroom."

Start small. Integration isn't a leap—it's a series of sacred steps back to yourself.

Speak this affirmation aloud, feeling it reverberate through every cell:

"I am one woman, indivisible, bringing heaven to earth through my leadership. My spirituality informs my strategy. My ancestry guides my authority. My wholeness is my power. I choose integration not as a practice but as a way of being. I am the bridge not between worlds but within myself—uniting all I am into all I'm becoming."

Feel the click of internal puzzle pieces finding their home. Feel the exhale of your soul, finally freed from the contortion of fragmentation. Feel the power that comes not from perfecting performance but from embracing presence.

You have passed through the four doorways. You have glimpsed what waits on the other side of fragmentation. But integration without protection becomes depletion. Your newly united self needs sacred boundaries to maintain its wholeness.

Turn the page when you're ready to learn the sacred art of protecting the unified sovereign you're becoming. Your boundaries aren't limitations—they're the architecture of your liberation.

4

The Sacred Art of Divine Boundaries

Boundaries aren't personal development luxury—they're spiritual technology.

Think of them as energy architecture. Just as a house needs walls to create sacred space within, your life needs boundaries to create a container for transformation. Without boundaries, your energy leaks everywhere, dispersing like water without a vessel. With them, you become a chalice capable of holding the sacred.

Quantum physics is clear: our energy fields extend beyond our physical bodies. When you operate without boundaries, you're not just tired—you're energetically hemorrhaging. Your aura becomes Swiss cheese, full of holes where other people's needs, expectations, and emotions rush in without invitation. No wonder you can't manifest. No wonder your prayers feel weak. You're trying to fill a bucket that has no bottom.

Boundaries as prayer: Each "no" is a "yes" to your divine assignment. You're declaring to the universe that you understand your energy is sacred currency.

Boundaries as altar: They create the sacred space where your transformation can unfold without interruption, where your gifts can develop without depletion.

Boundaries as medicine: They heal the ancestral wound of over-giving, treating the disease at its root rather than just managing symptoms.

Boundaries as legacy: Every boundary you set creates a new template in the collective field, making it easier for your daughters to protect their energy.

For Black women, boundary-setting isn't just personal—it's revolutionary. We're reversing centuries of conditioning that said our bodies, time, energy, and gifts were public property. We're declaring that the well of our wisdom has a gate, and we hold the key.

The Divine No is a complete sentence that requires no justification.

Learn the anatomy of a sacred refusal:

Pause: Before responding, breathe. Feel into your body. Is this a full-hearted yes or an obligated maybe?

Presence: Ground yourself in your sovereignty. You're not being mean. You're being aligned.

Purpose: Remember your divine assignment. Does this request serve your highest calling?

Power: Speak from your center, not your conditioning. Let your no come from love, not guilt.

Peace: Release attachment to their response. Your no is about your alignment, not their comfort.

"Thank you for thinking of me. This doesn't align with my current commitments."

"I'm honored you asked. My plate is beautifully full right now."

"I'm focusing my energy on specific priorities this season."

Watch what happens when you first start saying no. People who benefited from your boundarylessness will escalate—this is called an extinction burst. Like a child having a tantrum when candy is refused, they'll increase pressure to see if you'll cave. They'll call you selfish, difficult, "not a team player." They'll weaponize your care for them against you.

Dr. Sasha's family accused her of "acting brand new" when she stopped being available for every crisis. Her supervisor questioned her "commitment" when she stopped answering emails at midnight. But she held steady, breathing through the discomfort, remembering that her no was medicine they didn't know they needed.

"My no forced my family to discover their own strength," she reflected six months later. "My boundaries didn't destroy relationships—they revealed which ones were based on my depletion."

The somatic practice for holding boundaries: When you feel the guilt rising, place your hand on your heart. Breathe into that space. Say internally: "My boundary is a blessing. My no makes room for an aligned yes. I choose myself with love."

Energy protection for empathic leaders requires special consideration.

You feel everything. You walk into rooms and immediately sense who's struggling, who's angry, who needs what. Your mirror neurons are hyperactive, constantly picking up and processing others' emotions. This gift makes you a powerful leader—and energetically vulnerable.

Neuroscience is fascinating: empaths have more active mirror neuron systems, literally feeling others' experiences in their own bodies. Without protection, you become an emotional dumping ground, absorbing everyone's unprocessed pain.

Your Energy Protection Protocol:

Morning Armor: Before leaving home, visualize golden light surrounding you. Set the intention: "I am compassionately bound. I feel with others but don't take on their energy."

Meeting Shields: Before entering any meeting, touch a protective talisman (could be jewelry, a stone in your pocket). Activate your energetic boundary.

Clearing Rituals: Between interactions, shake your body, wash your hands while imagining energy flowing down the drain, and take three breaths to reset your field.

Weekly Restoration: Schedule non-negotiable restoration time. This isn't self-care—it's energy hygiene.

HR Director Naomi transformed her leadership when she learned energy protection. "I used to leave work feeling like I'd been hit by a truck. Everyone's problems lived in my body. Now I can hold space without becoming a storage unit for pain."

Boundaries don't make you less caring—they make you sustainably caring. You can't pour from an empty cup, but more importantly, you don't have to. Your emptiness serves no one. Your fullness serves everyone.

Begin your Boundary Temple construction with this 21-day practice:

Week 1 - Foundation (Days 1-7):

Identify your top three energy leaks

Notice without judgment where you say yes when you mean no

Practice one small no daily (start with low stakes)

Evening check-in: How did boundaries feel in your body today?

Week 2 - Walls (Days 8-14):

Set three non-negotiable boundaries (example: no calls after 8 PM)

Communicate these boundaries clearly

Hold steady through extinction bursts

Use somatic practices to stay centered

Celebrate each successful boundary hold

Week 3 - Roof (Days 15-21):

Implement advanced boundaries in challenging relationships

Practice energy protection in difficult environments

Create boundary rituals that feel sacred

Plan for long-term boundary maintenance

Ceremony on Day 21 to celebrate your temple

Common challenges you'll face:

The Guilt Spiral: "But they need me!" Remember: their need doesn't constitute your emergency. You're not responsible for being everyone's solution.

Family Pushback: "You've changed." Yes, you have. Evolution is the point. Hold steady with love.

Internal Resistance: Your conditioning will scream. Thank it for trying to protect you, then choose differently.

Share in the knowing: boundaries create ripples. As you protect your energy, others learn to manage their own. As you model sacred no's, you permit others to honor their limits. As you refuse to be depleted, you show your daughters that exhaustion isn't an inheritance.

Your boundaries give others permission to find their own strength.

This isn't selfishness—it's sacred modeling. Your sovereign boundaries declare to the universe that Black women's energy is precious, finite, and worthy of protection. You're not just setting personal boundaries—you're healing the collective pattern of depletion that has cost us too much for too long.

Stand now. Place both hands on your solar plexus, the seat of your personal power. Speak these three sacred boundaries aloud:

"I will no longer _____."

"I will protect my energy by _____."

"I choose to prioritize _____ without apology."

Feel the shift? That's your energy reorganizing around sustainable sovereignty. That's your ancestors celebrating that the pattern of depletion stops with you. That's your future self breathing easier because you chose to build boundaries instead of burnout.

Your exhaustion was never evidence of your worth. Your boundaries aren't evidence of your weakness. They're the architecture of a life that honors both your humanity and your divinity, your service and your sovereignty, your love for others and your sacred responsibility to yourself.

The throne you're building requires walls. Not to keep love out, but to keep power in. Not to separate you from community, but to ensure you have something sustainable to offer.

Your boundary temple awaits construction. Will you build?

5

Alchemy of the Wounded Healer

Let's map your sacred wounds.

Not to wallow, but to discover what medicine you're meant to make.

Take out paper. Create categories. Be honest about what still aches:

Invisibility Wounds: The times you were overlooked, erased, made transparent in rooms full of people who benefited from not seeing you. How many meetings were your contributions vanished? How many times did you watch your ideas bloom in someone else's garden?

Voice Wounds: Every interruption. Every time someone explained your own expertise to you. Every "actually" that preceded the dismantling of your knowing. The accumulated silence that calcified in your throat.

Worth Wounds: The promotion that went to someone less qualified but more "culturally aligned." The pay gap you discovered by accident. The moments you had to prove basic competence, while others' incompetence was presumed potential.

Identity Wounds: Being asked to speak for all Black women. Being told you're "not like other Black women" as if it were a compliment. The exhaustion of translating yourself for consumption by those who refuse to learn your language.

Trust Wounds: The mentor who took credit. The sponsor who disappeared when you needed backing. The sister who smiled in your face while undermining your rise. The moments that taught you that solidarity was conditional.

For each wound, ask: Is this still bleeding? Still fresh, still triggered by similar situations, still capable of hijacking your nervous system? This wound needs more healing before it can become medicine.

Is it scabbed? In process, tender but no longer gushing, able to be examined without falling apart? This wound is composting into wisdom.

Is it scarred? Healed but visible, integrated but not forgotten, transformed from wound to wisdom? This wound is ready for alchemy.

The difference between wallowing and alchemizing is consciousness. Wallowing keeps you stuck in the story of what happened to you. Alchemizing transforms you into the author of what happens next. One maintains you as a victim. The other initiates you as a healer.

You've been in mystery school all along.

Every Black woman leader walks a path that is both professional development and spiritual initiation. What you thought were career challenges were actually shamanic tests, each one designed to activate specific powers within you.

The Stripping: When everything you thought defined you was taken—title, position, false allies. This wasn't destruction but deconstruction, clearing space for who you really are.

The Void: That period where nothing made sense, where old strategies stopped working, where you felt suspended between who you were and who you were becoming. This wasn't emptiness but gestation.

The Remembering: When your spiritual gifts started breaking through your professional facade. When synchronicities became too frequent to ignore. When you realized your wounds had turned you into a metal detector for others' pain.

The Rising: Where you are now or approaching. When wound becomes wisdom, when personal healing becomes collective medicine, when your story becomes others' survival guide.

Folake knew her Wall Street trials were an initiation when she noticed the pattern. Every time she was about to level up, a specific type of attack would come—always questioning her competence despite her track record, always suggesting she was "too aggressive" when she was simply direct. The third time it happened, she laughed.

"I finally understood," she told me, eyes bright with recognition. "This wasn't random workplace toxicity. This was an initiation. Each attack was preparing me to hold more power by teaching me to source my worth from within. Now I run a healing center for women in finance. Every wound I sustained became a treatment I offer."

When you understand wounds as initiation, victimhood transforms into victory. You stop asking "Why me?" and start asking "What am I being prepared for?" You recognize that leaders who create real change are forged in real fire.

Now for the sacred work: transmutation.

For your Rage Wounds—those moments of injustice that still burn:

Create a Sacred Rage Ritual. Find a private space where you can move wildly, scream into pillows, beat drums, break things meant for breaking (thrift store plates against concrete walls make satisfying crashes). Let your body express what your professionalism had to contain. Then—this is crucial—channel that clarified rage into justice work. Start the program. Write the policy. Build the alternative. Rage without action is just fever. Rage with purpose is fuel.

For your Betrayal Wounds—those violations of trust that made you close:

Practice Trust Alchemy. Map what each betrayal taught you about discernment. That mentor who stole your work? She taught you to document. That ally who disappeared? She taught you the difference between performance and presence. Don't close your heart—refine your selection criteria. Transform naïveté into wisdom without losing capacity for connection.

For your Invisibility Wounds—the erasure that made you doubt your existence:

Reclaim Radiance. Create practices that take up space. Dance in your office with the door closed. Wear colors that refuse to apologize. Speak first in meetings. Post your wins. Document your journey. Become so visible that erasure becomes impossible. Not aggressive visibility—sovereign visibility. There's a difference.

Where do these wounds live in your body? Scan slowly from crown to root.

Voice wounds often lodge in the throat and jaw. Breathe blue light into these spaces, imagining calcified silence dissolving.

Worth wounds settle in the solar plexus. Place both hands here and breathe golden light, reclaiming your power center.

Trust wounds tighten the heart. Practice heart-opening poses, imagining green light creating space for discerning connection.

Some wounds transform quickly—a single ritual creating a permanent shift. Others require patient tending, like gardens that need seasons to show their beauty. Honor your timeline. This isn't work you complete but practice you embody.

The Medicine Making Protocol:

Identify the wound with specificity

Extract the wisdom (what did you learn?)

Clarify the medicine (how can this wisdom help others?)

Determine who needs it (who's bleeding where you've healed?)

Create delivery method (how will you share this medicine?)

You have healing gifts. Not metaphorically—literally.

People constantly share specific wounds with you because they sense you've alchemized that exact pain. You've navigated transformations others are struggling through. Wisdom flows effortlessly from your lived experience.

Which wounds do people bring to you repeatedly? This reveals your medicine specialty.

Are you the Voice Activator—the one who helps others speak their silenced truths?

The Worth Alchemist—transforming internalized inadequacy into unshakable value?

The Vision Keeper—holding others' dreams when they can't see past their current reality?

The Pattern Breaker—showing others how to disrupt generational cycles?

The Bridge Builder—creating a connection where separation seemed permanent?

Create your Healer-Leader Mission Statement: "I transform [specific wound] into [specific medicine] for [specific people] so that [specific liberation occurs]."

Example: "I transform the wound of stolen voice into the medicine of sovereign expression for Black women executives so that boardrooms become spaces of authentic power."

But remember the Wounded Healer's Code:

Transparency: Be honest about your ongoing healing. Perfection isn't required—consciousness is.

Boundaries: You can't heal everyone, especially those committed to staying wounded. Discern where your medicine will be received.

Continued Work: Keep tending your own wounds. Healed healers heal. Healing healers create more wounds.

Integration: Your professional role and healer identity aren't separate. Stop compartmentalizing your medicine.

Clean Pain Only: Help from processed pain creates liberation. Help from raw wounds creates codependence.

Dr. Ayana learned this distinction the hard way. "I was attracting the same type of toxic supervisor repeatedly. I thought I was healing others with similar experiences, but I was actually recreating my wound. Once I did my deep healing work, I stopped attracting those dynamics and started helping others transform theirs."

Now, create your Medicine Bundle.

Gather objects representing your journey from wound to wisdom. That rejection letter that redirected your path. The photo from the day you chose yourself. The certificate from the training your pain led you to pursue. The testimonial from someone your medicine helped heal.

Arrange these items consciously. Speak to each one: "Thank you for the medicine you helped me make." This isn't about glorifying pain but honoring transformation.

Create an activation ritual. Light a candle. State aloud: I am a wounded healer walking the sacred path of transformation. My wounds are not my shame but my initiation. My scars are not my limitation but my certification. I offer my medicine with clean hands and a conscious heart. I heal others as I continue healing myself. This is my sacred commitment."

Feel the circular connection—as you heal others, you continue healing yourself. Each person who receives your medicine validates that your journey wasn't in vain. Each wound that becomes wisdom proves that pain can have purpose without being purposefully inflicted.

Your medicine is unique because your wounds were specific. Your healing gifts are powerful because you know the territory of that exact suffering.

You didn't survive your wounds just to survive. You survived to help others transform theirs. You alchemized your pain to become someone's proof that transmutation is possible.

This is the sacred mathematics of the wounded healer: Your Pain × Conscious Transformation = Medicine∞

The wounds that once threatened to destroy you have become the medicine that defines your purpose. Not because pain is good, but because you are powerful enough to transform poison into cure.

Your medicine bundle is packed. Your healing gifts are activated. Your wounded healer mission is clear.

Who's waiting for exactly the medicine you've made?

6

Reclaiming Your Throne Room Voice

Speaking truth in spaces not designed for your voice requires strategy, not just courage.

Different throne rooms demand different approaches:

Corporate Boardrooms: Read the room's readiness before speaking. Build allies before meetings. Have data ready, but lead with vision. Position your truth as profitable innovation. Document everything. Create paper trails of your contributions.

Nonprofit Leadership: Frame truth in terms of mission alignment. Use storytelling to make points. Build coalitions before challenging systems. Expect resistance from those comfortable with the status quo.

Academic Spaces: Arm yourself with research, but don't hide behind it. Challenge intellectual supremacy with embodied knowing. Claim your expertise while honoring others'. Write your truth into existence—published words are harder to silence.

Political Arenas: Understand that truth here is always strategic. Time revelations for maximum impact. Build public support before private confrontations. Use media strategically. Remember: political spaces are theaters—perform accordingly.

Media Platforms: Control your narrative. Prepare key messages. Don't let others' questions limit your truth. Bridge to what needs saying. Remember: you're not just speaking to the interviewer but through them to your people.

The calculus Black women must do before speaking truth:

- What's the cost/benefit of this truth right now?
- Do I have the positional power to survive backlash?
- Are there allies who will amplify/support?
- Is this the hill I'm willing to die on?
- How can I speak truth while minimizing harm to myself?

Sometimes strategic silence serves your larger mission. Sometimes revolutionary truth-telling is required regardless of cost. Develop discernment through practice.

When your truth isn't received well:

- Document what you said and their response
- Find allies who heard/witnessed
- Don't internalize their resistance as your failure
- Remember: prophets are rarely popular in their time
- Trust that seeds planted grow even in hostile soil

Truth-telling isn't about being heard immediately but about planting seeds that grow over time. Your words create ripples beyond what you can see.

When queens speak from sovereignty, atmospheres shift.

Science confirms what ancestors knew: certain vocal frequencies literally change brainwaves in listeners. When you speak from your authentic power center, your voice carries a resonance that bypasses conscious resistance and speaks directly to others' nervous systems. This is why authentic voices create movements while performative ones create noise.

The Atmosphere Shifting Protocol:

Ground before speaking: Feel your feet on earth, your connection to something greater. You're not just speaking as yourself but as a channel for needed truth.

Set energetic intention: Before opening your mouth, internally declare your intention. "I speak for liberation." "I speak for clarity." Let that intention charge your words.

Speak from your power center: Not just your throat but your whole being. Let your voice originate from your core and flow through your heart before it reaches your lips.

Allow silence to amplify: After speaking powerful truth, don't rush to fill the silence. Let your words land, reverberate, do their work.

Track energy shifts: Notice how the room changes. Watch bodies relax or tense. Feel the atmospheric pressure shift. You're not imagining it—you're influencing the field.

Examples of atmosphere shifting in action:

The meeting is going nowhere until you say, "What if we're solving the wrong problem?" Suddenly, a real conversation begins.

The team stuck in fear until you share, "I've failed at this before. Here's what I learned." The room exhales. Permission to be human changes everything.

The negotiation stalled until you declared, "This isn't working for me." Your clarity creates movement.

With great vocal power comes great responsibility. Use your voice to elevate, not dominate. Create space for other voices while claiming your own. Remember: sovereign voice creates permission for others to find theirs.

Begin your voice restoration with this 13-day journey:

Days 1-3: Throat Chakra Healing

Morning: Gentle neck rolls while humming

Afternoon: Blue light meditation on the throat

Evening: Journal three unexpressed truths

Practice: Sing in the shower, hum while cooking, make sounds

Days 4-6: Reclaiming Ancestral Voices

Research how your grandmothers spoke

Listen to recordings of powerful Black women

Practice speaking affirmations in your ancestral tongue

Ritual: Light a blue candle, speak to your ancestors about reclaiming your voice

Days 7-9: Practicing Full Spectrum

Practice each voice type for 10 minutes

Record yourself using different voices

Use appropriate voice in real situations

Notice resistance and breathe through it

Days 10-12: Strategic Implementation

Choose one meeting to speak more truth

Practice your command voice in a safe space

Share one previously withheld insight

Document responses and results

Day 13: Integration Ceremony

Create sacred space

Review your journey

Speak your Voice Vow aloud

Commit to daily voice practices

Daily practices for maintained liberation:

Morning: Vocal warm-ups (humming, tongue twisters, scales)

Before speaking: Touch throat, connect to truth

Evening: Clear throat chakra with sound or song

Weekly: Use your full vocal range in some context

Create your Voice Vow:

"I vow to speak my truth with power and grace. I release all contracts of silence. I reclaim my full vocal range as birthright. I use my voice for liberation—my own and others'. My words create worlds. I speak, therefore I am free."

Your voice isn't just yours—it carries the silenced words of ancestors and creates pathways for descendants.

When we speak authentically, we heal the collective throat chakra of Black women. Each truth told makes the next one easier. Each voice reclaimed adds to the chorus that will eventually be impossible to silence.

Think of your daughters, your spiritual daughters, the young Black women watching you navigate these spaces. What do you want them to learn about their voices? That they must be hidden? Or that they are instruments of revolution when played in full?

Every time you drop your voice to its natural register, you give someone permission to find theirs. Every time you speak passionate truth in a boardroom, you expand what's possible. Every time you refuse to translate your knowing into pallid corporate-speak, you preserve medicine the world desperately needs.

The collective rising when we speak:

Meetings become spaces of authentic exchange

"Professionalism" expands to include full humanity

Young Black women enter workplaces where their voices are already valued

Truth becomes currency rather than liability

Systems transform because authentic voices demand authentic change

Stand now. Place one hand on your throat, one on your heart. Speak aloud:

"My voice is sacred. My truth is medicine. I speak for myself and for those who could not. I speak to heal and to liberate. I reclaim every octave, every tone, every expression that was taken from my lineage. I am the throat chakra healer my ancestors prayed for."

Feel the vibration of your own truth moving through your body. That resonance? That's power remembering itself. That's your voice coming home.

Your throne room awaits your true voice. Not the carefully modulated whisper you've been offering, but the full-spectrum symphony you were born to conduct.

The boardroom needs your bass notes. The strategy session needs your soprano insights. The negotiation needs your alto authority. All of you. All of your voices. All of your truth.

Speak, sovereign queen. The world is listening, even when it pretends not to hear.

Your voice changes everything. Use it.

7

The Mirror Work of Authentic Authority

The backlash is as predictable as it is painful.

When Dr. Samantha started leading with integrated authority, combining her business acumen with her spiritual wisdom, the resistance came in waves:

Tone Policing: "I'm concerned about how you came across in that meeting."

Translation: Your confidence is triggering my insecurity. The same assertiveness that gets others promoted gets Black women coached on "communication style."

Competence Questioning: Suddenly, work that was excellent last month needs "review."

Projects you've led successfully get "additional oversight." Your track record becomes invisible as they search for evidence to confirm their discomfort.

Isolation Tactics: The lunch invitations stop. The informal pre-meeting meetings happen without you.

They create an insider circle you're deliberately excluded from, hoping social pressure will make you conform.

Character Assassination: When other tactics fail, they attack your character. "Difficult." "Not a team player." "Aggressive." The coded language is designed to make you the problem rather than examining what your presence is revealing.

Subtle and Overt Retaliation: Passed over for opportunities. Removed from visible projects. Sometimes, even direct sabotage—files disappearing, emails "accidentally" not sent, your contributions mysteriously omitted from reports.

The Backlash Navigation Protocol:

Document Everything: Keep a sovereignty journal. Date, time, incident, witnesses. Not from paranoia but from wisdom. Your future self will thank you for the evidence trail.

Build Strategic Alliances: Find others who are ready for change. They exist—usually quieter, watching, waiting for someone to go first. Your authentic authority permits them to consider their own.

Manage Your Energy: Backlash is exhausting by design. Double down on your energy protection practices. This is spiritual warfare disguised as workplace dynamics.

Choose Battles Wisely: Not every slight needs a response. Not every aggression requires confrontation. Develop discernment about when to engage and when to let their resistance exhaust itself.

Maintain Perspective: Backlash often precedes breakthrough. The system fights hardest right before it changes. Their resistance is evidence of your impact.

Somatic practices for staying centered during backlash:

Before difficult meetings: Stand in power pose for two minutes, breathe into your core

When triggered: Feel your feet on the ground, touch a grounding object, remember who you are

After attacks: Shake your body to discharge their energy, take a salt bath, speak your truth to trusted allies

Remember: their reaction to your growth is information about their readiness, not validation of your worth.

Not all feedback is resistance. Developing sophisticated discernment is crucial.

The Discernment Matrix helps you evaluate feedback:

Source: Who's giving the feedback? Someone invested in your growth, or someone threatened by it? Someone with a track record of supporting Black women's advancement or someone who's been a gatekeeper?

Content: Is the feedback specific and actionable or vague and emotional? Does it address behavior that could genuinely improve your impact or attempt to diminish your authentic expression?

Pattern: Is this consistent feedback from multiple trusted sources or an isolated complaint from someone triggered by your transformation? Patterns reveal truth; isolated incidents often reveal projection.

Energy: How does the feedback feel in your body? Constructive feedback feels challenging but expansive. Resistance disguised as feedback feels constrictive, designed to make you smaller.

Outcome: What would happen if you integrated this feedback? Would you become more powerful yourself or return to a diminished version? Does it ask you to grow or shrink?

Dr. Keyana faced this discernment challenge when her manager said she was "coming on too strong" in meetings. She used the matrix:

Source: A manager known for preferring "collaborative" (aka passive) women

Content: Vague complaints about "energy", not specific behaviors

Pattern: Only happened after she started speaking first in meetings

Energy: Felt like a cage closing, not a door opening

Outcome: Following it would return her to an invisible support role

She thanked him for the feedback and continued showing up in her power. Six months later, she had his job.

But sometimes feedback is medicine:

When three trusted colleagues mentioned she seemed disconnected from the team, Dr. Michelle investigated. She realized her boundaries had become walls, her sovereignty had shifted to isolation. She adjusted—not abandoning her boundaries but creating more permeable ones that allowed for connection within protection. Her authority became more magnetic because it included rather than excluded.

Authentic authority includes the wisdom to know when flexibility serves sovereignty.

Every strong reaction to your authentic authority points to where they—and sometimes you—need integration.

When a colleague's dismissiveness triggers your impostor syndrome, notice. Their doubt found a pocket of self-doubt still living in you. This isn't failure—it's precision guidance showing exactly where to direct your healing attention.

The Trigger Transformation Process:

Identify the trigger: What specifically activated you? Their tone? Their words? Their dismissal?

Notice body response: Where did you feel it? Throat closing? Chest tightening? Stomach dropping?

Trace the root: When have you felt this before? What original wound is being touched?

Extract the lesson: What is this showing you about where you still need integration?

Integrate through practice: Create specific practices to heal this trigger point.

Example: Marketing director Zara noticed she was triggered whenever male colleagues interrupted her. Body scan revealed throat constriction and chest heat. She traced it to childhood dinner tables where her brothers' voices mattered more. The lesson: she still carried the belief that male voices held more weight. Her practice: speaking affirmations in her power voice daily, practicing not yielding the floor when interrupted.

Common trigger patterns for Black women leaders:

Being questioned triggers worthiness wounds

Being excluded triggers belonging wounds

Being criticized triggers perfectionism programming

Being unseen triggers invisibility trauma

Being misunderstood triggers exhaustion from translating

The paradox: as you grow stronger, triggers may initially intensify. Your system is upgrading, becoming more sensitive to what doesn't align. This isn't regression—it's refinement.

Those who trigger us most are often our greatest teachers in disguise, showing us exactly where we still have work to do.

Your authentic authority needs an ecosystem of support to thrive despite resistance.

Map your current ecosystem: Who amplifies your voice? Who challenges you to grow? Who undermines your authority? Who ignores your transformation? Who celebrates your becoming?

The Authority Ecosystem Architecture:

Mirrors: Other sovereign women who reflect your highest possibility. They see you clearly and call you forward into fuller expression. Find them in your organization, your industry, or adjacent spaces.

Anchors: Grounded souls who keep you connected to your why. They remind you of your purpose when backlash makes you question everything. Often, elders or spiritual advisors.

Expanders: People living beyond where you are, showing what's possible. They stretch your conception of authority and success. Follow them, learn from them, let them pull you forward.

Witnesses: Those who see and document your journey. They validate your experience when gaslighting makes you question reality. Crucial for Black women navigating spaces that deny our truth.

Co-creators: Aligned souls building new paradigms alongside you. They're not just supporting your authority but creating new systems where authentic authority thrives.

Building this ecosystem in predominantly white spaces requires creativity:

Look beyond your immediate environment

Build connections across industries

Find online communities of sovereign leaders

Create peer mentorship circles

Include ancestral support through spiritual practice

Dr. Asha built her ecosystem strategically: two mirrors in her company, an anchor in her spiritual advisor, expanders she followed online, witnesses in her Black women's leadership circle, and co-creators in her cross-industry innovation group. "I stopped expecting one workplace to provide all my support. I built a constellation that could hold my whole becoming."

Gracefully release toxic connections while building supportive ones. Not everyone from your "before" can journey to your "after." Some relationships were built on your diminishment and can't survive your sovereignty. Release with love, but release nonetheless.

Mirror work accelerates your evolution exponentially.

Every external challenge that mirrors internal work creates an opportunity for quantum leap growth. It's spiritual CrossFit—intense but transformative. The universe uses mirrors to show us what we can't see ourselves, to refine us faster than solo work ever could.

When someone's doubt mirrors your hidden self-doubt, healing that doubt heals both internal and external patterns. When someone's resistance mirrors your own resistance to being seen, breaking through serves both your liberation and theirs.

Dr. Carmen's story illustrates this acceleration. Her manager's constant questioning of her intuitive insights mirrored her own distrust of her knowing. Instead of just fighting him, she did deep work on trusting her intuition. As she healed internally, his resistance mysteriously decreased. "I realized he was just playing the role my own doubt had cast him in. When I trusted myself, he had to find a new part to play."

The spiritual principle: the universe uses mirrors to show us what needs healing, and healing it changes the entire reflection.

Create a celebration practice for honoring difficult mirrors as sacred teachers. When someone triggers you profoundly:

Thank them internally for showing you where you're not free

Do your healing work around what they revealed

Watch how the dynamic shifts as you integrate

Celebrate the growth their resistance catalyzed

Authentic authority isn't about everyone accepting you—it's about you accepting yourself so fully that others' reactions become information rather than definition.

Stand before your bathroom mirror. Look into your own eyes—the first and most important mirror. Place your hand on your heart and speak:

"I am a sacred mirror reflecting truth, possibility, and choice. I welcome the reflections that show me where to grow. I release attachment to others' comfort with my authority. I trust that my authentic presence serves the highest good, even when it disrupts the familiar. I am worthy of being seen in my full power."

Feel the shift? That's you claiming your role as both mirror and sovereign—reflecting truth while standing unmoved by others' reactions to that truth.

The mirror work of authentic authority isn't always comfortable, but it's always transformative. Every reflection you create, every reaction you catalyze, every resistance you meet is part of the sacred choreography of collective evolution.

Your authentic authority is a gift, even to those who initially reject it. You're showing them that another way is possible. You're creating cracks in the facades they've built. You're planting seeds that will bloom in their own time.

Stand firm in your authority, sovereign queen. The mirrors you create are medicine this world desperately needs.

8

Dancing with Resistance and Revelation

Map the types of resistance as power indicators:

Systemic Resistance: When policies suddenly need "review," when budgets mysteriously shrink, when bureaucracy multiplies around your initiatives. This means you're threatening institutional patterns.

Power indicator: You're creating change at structural levels.

Interpersonal Resistance: When relationships shift, alliances dissolve, and previously supportive colleagues become distant or hostile. This indicates you're disrupting social hierarchies.

Power indicator: You're modeling new ways of being that challenge comfortable dynamics.

Internal Resistance: When your own conditioning screams louder, when impostor syndrome flares, when old patterns fight for survival. This signals a deep transformation.

Power indicator: You're breaking ancestral patterns and creating new templates.

Energetic Resistance: When you feel unseen forces working against you, when obstacles appear supernatural in their timing, when you sense pushback from the collective field.

Power indicator: You're shifting paradigms at quantum levels.

Black women face amplified resistance because we're not supposed to have sovereign power in systems built on our subjugation. Our authentic authority doesn't just challenge workplace dynamics—it challenges the foundational myths these systems depend on.

When we lead from wholeness, we expose the lie that exploitation is necessary for success. When we thrive authentically, we prove that power can heal rather than harm.

Your resistance is proportional to your purpose. The bigger your mission, the bigger the pushback. Consider it a cosmic compliment.

Resistance isn't your enemy—it's your intelligence officer, providing precise data about where to focus your evolution.

The Resistance Oracle System reveals specific guidance:

Immediate, Emotional Resistance: You've hit a core wound—theirs or yours. When reaction is instant and charged with emotion disproportionate to your action, you've touched something primal. This resistance says: "There's deep healing needed here."

Navigation: Slow down but don't stop. Breathe through the charge. Get curious about what sacred wound you've activated. Often, this is where the greatest transformation waits.

Delayed, Strategic Resistance: You've threatened power structures. When resistance comes after meetings, through formal channels, with calculated precision, you've disrupted systems that benefit from current dysfunction. This resistance says: "You're playing at levels that matter."

Navigation: Document everything. Build strategic alliances. Play the long game. This isn't personal—it's chess. Make moves that protect your position while advancing your mission.

Scattered, Unfocused Resistance: You're creating chaos in stagnant systems. When resistance seems to come from everywhere and nowhere, when it's more atmosphere than attack, you're stirring waters that have been still too long. This resistance says: "Change is beginning whether they're ready or not."

Navigation: Stay centered in your purpose. Let the chaos swirl without joining it. Be the eye of the storm. Your groundedness will eventually reorganize the entire field.

The somatic art of reading resistance: Your body knows before your mind. Immediate resistance often feels like solar plexus activation—power recognizing power. Strategic resistance registers as third eye pressure—your intuition alerting you to hidden agendas. Scattered resistance feels like static electricity—energy fields in conflict.

Dr. Nadia developed mastery in reading resistance: "I started treating pushback like weather reports. Storm coming from the northeast? That's the finance department feeling threatened. High pressure from above? Leadership is nervous about my influence. Once I stopped taking it personally and started reading it strategically, I could navigate anything."

The 48-Hour Oracle Practice: When facing resistance, wait 48 hours before responding. Use that time to read the deeper message. Your first reaction is usually ego. Your second response is wisdom.

Think of yourself as an alkaline presence in acidic environments.

The science: alkaline substances neutralize acids without becoming acidic themselves. You can transform toxic resistance without absorbing it. This isn't about being unaffected—it's about being differently affected.

Your Sovereign Alkaline Protocol:

Morning Fortification (10 minutes):

- Stand barefoot on earth if possible
- Breathe golden light into your energy field
- Speak your daily intention: "I transform all resistance into fuel for my mission."
- Visualize yourself surrounded by protective alkaline light
- Seal your field with a gesture that feels powerful

Interaction Alchemy (ongoing):

- Before entering challenging spaces, touch your power talisman
- When resistance arises, breathe into your core
- Mentally note: "This is information, not definition."
- Imagine their acid hitting your alkaline and transforming
- Stay connected to your purpose, not their provocation

Evening Restoration (15 minutes):

- Shake your body to release absorbed energy
- Take a salt bath with the intention of clearing
- Journal what resistance revealed about your growth edge
- Thank the resistance for its teaching
- Replenish your alkaline reserves through prayer/meditation

Weekly Deep Cleanse (1 hour):

- Comprehensive energy clearing ritual
- Review the week's resistance patterns
- Extract wisdom from each challenge
- Reset your energetic template
- Celebrate your alkaline victories

Different toxicity types require different approaches:

Passive-Aggressive Undermining: The smile that hides sabotage. They agree in meetings, then obstruct in practice. Alkaline response: Document agreements. Follow up in writing. Make invisible visible.

Direct Character Assassination: Attacks on your credibility, competence, or character. Alkaline response: Let your work speak. Build undeniable track records. Their lies can't stand against your evidence.

Systemic Sabotage: Structural impediments designed to ensure failure. Alkaline response: Become forensically strategic. Anticipate obstacles. Create alternative pathways. Use their system against itself.

The Toxicity Transmutation Practice: Visualize the negative energy directed at you entering your field and being transformed by your alkaline presence into pure potential. See yourself as an energy recycling plant—taking their toxic waste and converting it into fuel for your mission.

Dr. Keisha mastered this during a brutal acquisition: "The new leadership tried everything to push me out. I started visualizing their attacks as coal being pressurized into diamonds by my alkaline field. By the end, I had enough diamonds to build my own company. Their resistance literally became my resources."

Sovereign leadership includes sovereign timing.

Not every truth needs immediate expression. Not every vision requires instant unveiling. Strategic revelation means knowing when your truth will have maximum impact versus maximum backlash.

The Revelation Strategy Matrix:

Consider four factors:

- Readiness of Audience: Are they prepared to receive this truth?
- Your Positional Power: Can you survive the potential backlash?
- Available Allies: Who will amplify and support your revelation?
- Mission Timing: Does revealing now serve your larger purpose?

Map your revelation through Seven Gateways:

- Gateway 1 - Personal Circle: Share with trusted intimates who provide a safe practice space
- Gateway 2 - Peer Allies: Reveal to equals who can offer strategic support
- Gateway 3 - Team Testing: Introduce concepts to direct reports/collaborators
- Gateway 4 - Organizational Soft Launch: Present ideas in low-stakes contexts
- Gateway 5 - Formal Channels: Bring revelation through official pathways
- Gateway 6 - Public Platform: Share with broader professional community
- Gateway 7 - Thought Leadership: Become a visible voice for transformation

The specific calculus for Black women: We face unique considerations. Our revelations get labeled "angry" when they're truthful, "aggressive" when they're assertive. Calculate carefully, but don't let calculation become paralysis.

Dr. Aisha navigated this brilliantly: "I spent six months planting seeds before revealing my full vision. By the time I presented formally, half the organization was already bought in through conversations they thought were casual. My revolution looked like evolution to them."

Creating revelation timelines:

Month 1-2: Personal integration and trusted circle

Month 3-4: Strategic ally building

Month 5-6: Soft launch and testing

Month 7-8: Formal presentation

Months 9-12: Full implementation and thought leadership

Remember: Sovereign timing isn't hiding—it's strategic unveiling for maximum impact and minimum harm.

Master the martial art of transformation—using oppositional energy to accelerate your mission.

Aikido principles translated to leadership:

Never Meet Force with Force: When they attack your credibility, don't defend—demonstrate. When they question your methods, don't argue—show results. Use their energy against itself.

Redirect Rather Than Block: Blocking creates collision. Redirecting uses their momentum for your purpose. They say you're "too ambitious"? Redirect: "I am ambitious—for this organization's highest potential."

Find the Void: In Aikido, you step where they aren't. In leadership, innovate where they're not looking. While they guard the front door, transform the foundation.

Specific redirection techniques:

The Question Flip: They ask, "Who authorized this change?" You respond, "What results would make this change worthwhile to you?" You've redirected from permission to possibility.

The Evidence Mount: They claim your approach won't work. You present three pilot programs already showing success. Their skepticism becomes your platform for proof.

The Alliance Build: They try to isolate you. You create connections they didn't expect—across departments, industries, hierarchies. Their attack becomes your networking catalyst.

The Innovation Catalyst: They resist your ideas. You frame them as experiments with measurable outcomes. Their resistance becomes a reason for controlled innovation.

Dr. Sophia became an Aikido master: "When the board said my vision was 'too radical,' I thanked them for recognizing its transformative potential and asked which parts excited them most. I used their own words—radical transformation—as the benchmark for success. By year-end, they were bragging about supporting radical innovation."

Energy conservation through Aikido: Fighting exhausts you. Redirecting energizes you. Every successful redirect builds your power while depleting theirs. You're not working harder—you're working physics.

Advanced practice: Gratitude for resistors as unconscious collaborators. They're showing you exactly where the system is weakest, exactly where transformation can enter.

Transform your resistance navigation from concept to daily practice with this 30-day sprint:

Week 1 - Resistance Recognition (Days 1-7):

Daily log: What resistance did I face? What type was it?

Evening reflection: What power indicator does this represent?

Practice: Thank each resistance internally for revealing your impact

Track patterns: What triggers most resistance in your environment?

Week 2 - Reading the Oracle (Days 8-14):

Implement a 48-hour pause before responding to resistance

Journal the deeper message in each pushback

Practice somatic resistance reading

Notice what resistance reveals about growth edges

Weekly review: What intelligence did resistance provide?

Week 3 - Alkaline Mastery (Days 15-21):

Full Sovereign Alkaline Protocol daily

Track energy levels before/after challenging interactions

Practice toxicity transmutation in real-time

Document how your alkaline presence shifts dynamics

Celebrate each successful neutralization

Week 4 - Strategic Dancing (Days 22-30):

Apply aikido principles to one challenge daily

Practice strategic revelation in low-stakes situations

Use redirection techniques in meetings

Build evidence of how resistance accelerates the mission

Day 30: Ceremony acknowledging resistance as a teacher

Integration practices for each day:

Morning: Set intention for dancing with resistance

Midday: Quick alkaline reset (2 minutes)

Evening: Journal one resistance transformed into a resource

Weekly: Share victories with accountability partner

Your mastery of resistance creates ripple effects:

When others see you transform pushback into power, they learn it's possible. Your grace under fire becomes their permission to stay centered. Your strategic navigation shows them pathways they couldn't see. You become living proof that resistance doesn't have to mean retreat.

Dr. Maya's team watched her navigate brutal resistance during a merger: "She turned every attack into an opportunity to demonstrate our value. By the end, the people trying to eliminate our department were fighting to fund us. She didn't just survive—she showed us how to alchemize opposition into opportunity."

Connect your personal mastery to collective transformation. Every time you transform resistance into fuel, you weaken its power in the collective field. You're not just changing your experience—you're changing the game itself.

Resistance isn't your enemy but your dance partner in the choreography of transformation.

Stand in your power stance. Feel the ground beneath you, the ancestors behind you, the vision before you. Speak aloud:

"I am a sovereign leader who dances with resistance and transforms it into revelation. Every pushback accelerates my purpose. Every obstacle becomes my opportunity. I am alkaline in acidic environments, Aikido master in conflict, a strategic revealer of necessary truths. Resistance is my teacher, my fuel, my confirmation that I'm creating real change."

Feel that shift? That's you claiming mastery over the very forces meant to stop you. That's you recognizing resistance as the honor it is—confirmation that your transformation is too powerful to ignore.

The dance continues, but now you know the steps. Each spin of resistance becomes your opportunity to demonstrate grace. Each dip of challenge lets you show your flexibility. Each leap over obstacles proves your readiness for flight.

Dance on, sovereign queen. The resistance can't resist your rhythm forever.

9

Building Your Sacred Constellation

The Sacred Seven framework isn't about finding seven people — it's about ensuring seven functions are fulfilled in your support ecosystem.

The Mirror (reflects your highest self): This soul sees your divine potential even when you're covered in the dust of daily struggle. They don't buy your small stories or limiting beliefs. When you say "I can't," they remind you of when you did. When you forget your queendom, they address you as royalty until you remember.

Finding Your Mirror: Look for someone who celebrates your growth rather than mourns your changes. Often, someone who's walked similar paths but slightly ahead. They see you becoming because they've become.

Cultivation: Regular check-ins where you share your edge—where you're growing, struggling, evolving. Ask them to reflect on what they see. Give them permission to call you higher.

The Anchor (grounds you): When sovereignty work has you floating in spiritual realms or spinning in mental stratospheres, your Anchor pulls you back to earth. They remind you to eat when you're consumed by vision, to rest when you're intoxicated by purpose, to laugh when you're taking yourself too seriously.

Finding Your Anchor: Often an earth sign friend, a practical soul who loves your magic but keeps your feet on the ground. Someone unimpressed by titles but devoted to your well-being.

Cultivation: Include them in practical decisions. Share your human moments, not just highlights. Let them tend to your earthly needs without shame.

The Oracle (speaks truth): This soul delivers divine downloads and human honesty with equal precision. They'll tell you when you're out of alignment, when you're playing small, when you're fooling yourself. Their truth sometimes stings, but always liberates.

Finding Your Oracle: Look for someone whose own life demonstrates integrated wisdom. Often, an elder or someone who's survived what you're navigating. Truth-tellers who love you too much to let you stay stuck.

Cultivation: Create agreements about truth-telling. Ask specific questions. Receive their medicine even when it's bitter. Thank them for loving you enough to risk your comfort.

The Strategist (helps navigate): This brilliant mind helps you play chess while others play checkers. They see systems, anticipate obstacles, and design pathways. When you're too close to see clearly, they provide an eagle-eye perspective on your battlefield.

Finding Your Strategist: Often someone in or adjacent to your field with complementary genius. They think in ways that expand your own strategic capacity. Natural systems thinkers who enjoy complex problem-solving.

Cultivation: Regular strategy sessions. Share your challenges early, not just when a crisis hits. Include them in vision planning. Honor their intellectual contribution.

The Healer (tends wounds): This soul helps you process and release what accumulates in leadership trenches. They might be formal healers—therapists, energy workers, or natural healers who create space for your unwinding.

Finding Your Healer: Someone who holds space without trying to fix. One who can witness your pain without drowning in it. Often have their own healing practice or deep personal healing journey.

Cultivation: Regular tending, not just crisis intervention. Share the tender places. Let them help you maintain, not just recover. Create rituals of renewal together.

The Catalyst (pushes growth): This soul won't let you settle. They see your edge and lovingly push you toward it. When you're comfortable, they create sacred discomfort. They believe in your capacity more than you do.

Finding Your Catalyst: Often, someone who intimidates you slightly with their own audacity. They're living at levels you aspire to. Natural change agents who can't help but inspire evolution.

Cultivation: Share your biggest visions. Ask them to hold you accountable. When they push, breathe through resistance, and lean in. Thank them for refusing to let you be mediocre.

The Witness (holds space): This soul provides unconditional presence. They don't need you to be anything other than what you are in each moment. With them, you can fall apart without fear, celebrate without explanation, and exist without performance.

Finding Your Witness: Someone with a profound capacity for presence. Often quieter souls who listen with their whole being. They create sanctuary through their attention.

Cultivation: Spend unstructured time together. Share stream of consciousness. Practice being rather than doing in their presence. Let them see all your faces.

Remember: One person might fulfill multiple roles. Your child might be a Witness. Your ancestor might be your Oracle. Your journal might be your Mirror. Not all support comes in human form.

Sister Circles transcend networking. They're cauldrons of collective alchemy.

Dr. Keyana's Sister Circle began when she realized conference "networking" left her emptier than before. "I had 500 LinkedIn connections and zero soul connections. I could get a meeting with anyone, but had no one to call when I needed to hear 'me too.'"

She started with three women—one from her company, one from her spiritual community, one from her gym. The only requirements: mutual commitment to growth, willingness to be vulnerable, shared understanding that their rising was collective.

The Sister Circle Alchemy Formula:

Shared Values + Vulnerability + Consistency + Sacred Container = Transformation

Creating your own Sister Circle:

Identifying Souls: Look for resonance over resume. Seek women who trigger your growth edge. Diversity of experience, unity of purpose. 3-7 members are optimal for intimacy.

Establishing Agreements: Confidentiality is non-negotiable. What's shared in circle stays in circle. Commitment to consistency—a missing circle requires a real reason. No advice unless requested. Celebration as important as problem-solving.

Creating Rituals: Open with grounding—meditation, prayer, or breathing. Check-ins that go beyond surface. Themed discussions: boundaries, money, relationships, purpose. Close with gratitude and commitments.

Common challenges and solutions:

Scheduling: Choose a sacred time and protect it fiercely

Ego dynamics: Address directly when they arise

Unequal sharing: Create a structure ensuring everyone speaks

Energy vampires: Lovingly release those who only take

Beyond human circles, you have Soul Councils—your personal board of directors, including ancestors, archetypes, and guides. Dr. Aisha's council includes her grandmother, Maya Angelou, the goddess Oshun, and her future self. She consults them in meditation before major decisions.

Circles are revolutionary acts reclaiming the collective power that isolation stole.

Building support when you're "the only one" requires creative strategies.

The exhaustion of being the sole Black woman in leadership can make support feel impossible. You're tired of educating, translating, and code-switching even in supposedly supportive spaces. You need mirrors that recognize you without explanation.

Strategic approaches:

Cross-Industry Connections: Your mirrors might not be in your building or even your field. Dr. Sasha found her constellation through a Black women's leadership conference.

"My support team includes a judge, a surgeon, and a tech founder. We understand each other's challenges without sharing industries."

Virtual Villages: Online communities provide 24/7 access to collective wisdom. Private Facebook groups, Marco Polo threads, Slack channels become lifelines. Geography doesn't limit sovereignty support.

Ancestral Advisory: When human support feels lacking, ancestral connection provides profound holding. Create an altar space for ancestral consultation.

Journal conversations with grandmothers. Feel their presence in challenging moments.

Strategic Vulnerability: Test potential supporters with small vulnerabilities before sharing deeper truths. Notice who handles your humanity with grace. Build slowly but steadily.

The Ally Assessment Protocol for predominantly white spaces:

Observe actions over words: Who amplifies Black women's voices? Who shares power/resources?

Test with small truths: Share minor challenges and observe response

Watch patterns: Do they consistently show up or only when convenient?

Energy check: Do you feel more or less yourself after interactions?

Reciprocity reality: Do they also show vulnerability or just consume yours?

Creative solutions that work:

Monthly virtual moon circles with Black women across time zones

Peer mentorship pods—3-4 women at similar levels supporting each other

Voxer groups for daily voice message support

Annual retreats that fill your cup for months

Professional development as a community-building opportunity

Sustainable support requires balanced energy exchange.

The Spiritual Law of Reciprocity isn't about scorekeeping—it's about conscious flow.

Energy, like water, must circulate to stay fresh. Stagnant support becomes an obligation, then becomes resentment, before it becomes destruction.

Common imbalances to address:

Overgiving: You pour endlessly without receiving. Often stems from worthiness wounds—believing you must earn support through depletion. Creates martyrdom and burnout.

Underreceiving: You deflect support, minimize needs, and refuse help. Usually, protection against disappointment or control issues. Creates isolation and exhaustion.

Taking Without Giving: You consume others' energy without reciprocal flow. Sometimes unconscious, learned from scarcity. Creates karmic debt and relationship destruction.

The Reciprocity Reset Process:

Audit Current Exchanges: List key relationships. For each, note what you give/receive. Include energy, time, resources, expertise, and emotional support. Notice patterns without judgment.

Identify Imbalances: Where are you overgiving? Underreceiving? Taking without returning? Be specific. Often, we give what we want to give, not what others need.

Have Conscious Conversations: "I've noticed our exchanges feel imbalanced. I value our connection and want to explore how we can create more reciprocity." Direct but loving.

Establish New Agreements: Be specific about needs and capacities. "I can offer monthly strategy sessions. I need accountability check-ins." Clear agreements prevent resentment.

Regular Reassessment: Quarterly check-ins about balance. Relationships evolve; agreements should, too.

Creative Reciprocity Beyond Money:

Skill exchanges—your strategy for their design

Energy exchanges—their healing session for your workshop

Access exchanges—your network introduction for their platform share

Wisdom exchanges—your experience for their innovation

Time exchanges—your focused attention for their project support

Dr. Nicole transformed her support ecosystem through reciprocity reset: "I realized I was overgiving professionally while underreceiving personally. I started asking for help with life logistics in exchange for business mentoring. Balance changed everything."

Balanced reciprocity creates sustainable support. You deserve to receive as generously as you give.

Activate your constellation through ceremony:

Choose a date aligned with a new or full moon. Gather:

Seven candles representing the Sacred Seven functions

Paper and pen for declarations

Tokens representing current and desired support

Music that moves your spirit

The Ceremony:

Opening: Create sacred space through prayer, sage, or sound. Call in your highest self and helping spirits.

Acknowledgment: Light candles for current supporters, speaking gratitude for each. Include human and non-human support. Honor even imperfect support as teaching.

Visioning: Write your constellation vision. Who do you call in? What support do you require? Be specific about qualities and functions needed.

Declaration: Speak aloud your commitment to conscious constellation building: "I release the myth of solo success. I am open to sacred support. I commit to balanced reciprocity. I trust the right souls will find me as I find them."

Integration: Create three action steps: one person to reach out to, one boundary to set, and one reciprocity conversation to have.

Closing: Thank all beings who participated. Blow out candles, sending wishes for collective support to all sovereign leaders.

Integration practices for sustained support:

Daily: Morning gratitude for one supporter

Weekly: Reach out to one constellation member

Monthly: Assess energy exchanges and adjust

Quarterly: Sister Circle or Soul Council meeting

Annually: Constellation mapping and ceremony

You are not meant to lead alone. Your sovereignty includes knowing you are worthy of sacred support.

The queens whose names echo through history didn't rule in isolation. They had advisors, priestesses, sister queens, and divine councils. Your queendom deserves no less. Your mission requires sustainable support. Your heart needs to be witnessed holding. Your vision demands collective manifestation.

Release the myth that needing others diminishes your power. In truth, trying to do everything alone is a diminishment. It keeps you small, exhausted, and controllable. Building conscious community is a revolutionary act—for you and every woman watching you model another way.

Your constellation awaits. Some souls are already in your orbit, waiting for an invitation closer. Others are seeking you as you seek them. Trust the magnetic pull of aligned support. Trust that as you clarify your needs, the universe conspires to meet them.

You are worthy of a constellation that celebrates your light, holds your shadow, and amplifies your sovereign power. Build it like your legacy depends on it—because it does.

Stand beneath the night sky. Feel the vast web of connection—stars supporting stars, galaxies held by galaxies. You are part of this cosmic constellation. Never alone. Always held. Forever connected.

Your sacred support constellation is assembling. Open your arms and let them in.

10

Designing Your Liberation Legacy

To architect conscious legacy, you must first heal the leadership wounds carried in our collective bloodline.

Map the historical patterns encoded in our DNA: Brilliance forced underground during slavery when literacy meant death. Leadership expressed only in spaces white supremacy couldn't reach—churches, kitchens, healing circles.

Innovations stolen and credited to others, from Henrietta Lacks to Katherine Johnson to countless unnamed ancestors whose genius built this country while being denied its benefits. Voices silenced by violence, both physical and psychological.

These wounds manifest in our bodies now as:

Imposter syndrome that's actually an ancestral memory of being punished for excellence

Overwork is an inherited survival strategy from ancestors who had to prove their worth through exhaustion

The compulsion to document everything because our contributions have been erased

Voice modulation that carries the cellular memory of code-switching for survival

The exhaustion of representation, carrying our entire race on our shoulders in every room

You stand at the sacred crossroads where historical wounds meet future healing. Your sovereignty isn't just personal recovery—it's ancestral redemption.

Create your Lineage Leadership Healing Protocol:

Identify Your Family's Leadership Wound: What specific pattern runs through your maternal line? Perhaps the women in your family led from shadows, powerful but uncredited.

Maybe they sacrificed their dreams to ensure survival. Or they learned to channel leadership through acceptable roles—teachers, nurses, mothers—never CEOs or senators.

Honor What It Protected: These patterns weren't failures—they were survival strategies. Your grandmother's silence protected her from violence. Your mother's overwork ensured economic stability. Honor the protection before releasing the pattern.

Declare What You'll Heal: Write and speak aloud: "The women in my lineage led from shadows. I lead from light. The pattern of hidden power ends with me. I heal this wound for all of us—past, present, and future."

Envision the New Pattern: See your daughter, niece, or spiritual daughters leading without apology. Imagine them never questioning their right to power, never dimming their light, never fragmenting their wholeness. Feel how your healing creates their freedom.

Perform a ritual for your ancestors. Light candles for each generation you can name. Speak to them directly: "Thank you for surviving so I could thrive. Thank you for your hidden leadership that preserved our lineage.

I honor your choices and choose differently. Watch me heal what you couldn't. This is for all of us."

As you heal these wounds, you literally change the morphic field—that invisible but real energetic template that influences behavior across generations. Your healing creates new possibilities not just for your direct descendants but for all Black women navigating leadership.

You embody specific Liberation Leader Archetypes that determine how your legacy manifests.

The Gateway Opener creates access where barriers existed. You're the first Black woman VP, the only one in the boardroom, the pioneer in your field. Your very presence opens doors, but you go further—you dismantle the locks. You create programs, policies, and pathways, ensuring you're not the last.

Leadership Style: Strategic barrier removal. You see systems; others accept and transform them.

Impact Pattern: Geometric progression—each door you open allows multiple others through.

Shadow to Watch: Burnout from carrying the weight of "first and only."

Practice for Embodiment: Weekly ritual acknowledging doors opened, monthly strategy session for systemic access creation.

The Pattern Destroyer dismantles toxic systems from within. You recognize dysfunctional patterns that others normalize and systematically disrupt them. Was that meeting culture built on interruption and dominance? You transform it. The unspoken rule that Black women must work twice as hard for half the recognition? You expose and explode it.

Leadership Style: Sacred disruption with strategic precision.

Impact Pattern: Catalytic—your disruptions force system-wide reckonings.

Shadow to Watch: Becoming so focused on destruction, you forget to build.

Practice for Embodiment: Balance every pattern destroyed with a new pattern created.

The Wisdom Keeper preserves and transmits cultural knowledge that systems try to erase. You document our ways of knowing, create archives of our innovations, and ensure our stories survive. You understand that keeping our wisdom alive is revolutionary in a world designed for our amnesia.

Leadership Style: Teaching through being, preserving through practice.

Impact Pattern: Generational—your preserved wisdom guides decisions decades later.

Shadow to Watch: Hoarding wisdom instead of circulating it.

Practice for Embodiment: Monthly wisdom-sharing circles, annual documentation projects.

The Bridge Builder connects worlds that seem separate. You translate between spiritual and corporate, between grassroots and grasstops, between ancient wisdom and modern innovation. Your bilingual soul helps others find connection where they saw only separation.

Leadership Style: Diplomatic alchemy, creating unexpected alliances.

Impact Pattern: Network effects—your bridges become highways for collective travel.

Shadow to Watch: Losing yourself in translation, forgetting your own native tongue.

Practice for Embodiment: Regular grounding in your primary world while building bridges to others.

The Future Weaver imagines and manifests possibilities others can't yet see. You're the visionary who dreams new systems into being, who articulates futures so compelling that others reorganize their present to reach them. Your imagination becomes a collective destination.

Leadership Style: Prophetic architecture, building tomorrow today.

Impact Pattern: Magnetic pull—your visions draw resources and souls toward manifestation.

Shadow to Watch: Frustration when others can't see what's obvious to you.

Practice for Embodiment: Vision boarding for collective futures, patience practices for divine timing.

Take time to identify your primary and secondary archetypes. Notice which descriptions create body resonance, which shadow warnings feel familiar. You might embody Gateway Opener primarily with Future Weaver rising. This self-knowledge focuses your legacy creation—not scattered impact but concentrated transformation.

Now architect your Liberation Blueprint with the precision of a master builder.

Vision: In 2050, what exists because you lived and led? Be specific. Perhaps: "A global network of spiritually integrated Black women CEOs who've transformed capitalism from extraction to regeneration." Or: "Educational systems that honor multiple intelligences and cultural ways of knowing." Or: "Healing centers in every major city where Black women restore their sovereignty." Write your 2050 vision in the present tense, as if reporting from that future.

Mission: Your mission bridges current reality to future vision. Example: "To create and model spiritually integrated leadership that heals while it succeeds, transforming every institution I touch into spaces where Black women thrive authentically."

Values: What principles guide your liberation leadership?

Authenticity over assimilation

Collective rise over individual climb

Spiritual integration over fragmentation

Sustainable power over burnout

Truth-telling over peacekeeping

Strategies: How will you manifest this liberation?

Interpersonal: Mentoring 100 Black women into senior leadership

Organizational: Transforming hiring, promotion, and culture policies

Systemic: Publishing work that shifts academic discourse

Cultural: Creating media that normalizes Black women's sovereignty

Metrics: How will you measure liberation impact?

Number of Black women promoted after your mentorship

Policy changes that create systemic access

Shifted organizational cultures (measured by retention, satisfaction, advancement)

Multiplier effects—how many others create similar changes

Timeline: Map liberation milestones:

Year 1: Internal transformation and small-scale modeling

Year 3: Organizational influence and initial system disruption

Year 5: Industry recognition and expanded platform

Year 10: National influence and policy impact

Year 20: International legacy and generational transformation

Sign and date your Liberation Blueprint as a sacred contract with yourself, your ancestors, and your descendants.

The mathematics of liberation multiplication will astound you.

If you liberate yourself fully and inspire just 10 other Black women to do the same, and each of them inspires 10, within three generations, that's 1,000 sovereign Black women leading from wholeness. But the mathematics go deeper.

Each sovereign Black woman leader impacts a minimum:

5 family members who witness her transformation

20 colleagues who experience her different way of leading

50 community members touched by her expanded service

100 annual interactions where her sovereignty shifts dynamics

Your Liberation × 10 women = 100 directly impacted

Those 100 × 10 each = 1,000 in second wave

Those 1,000 × 10 each = 10,000 in third wave

Within a decade, your personal sovereignty journey will influence 10,000 lives. This isn't inspiration math—it's documented social network theory. But for Black women, the multiplication carries an extra charge because we are influenced from positions of hypervisibility. When we transform, entire fields shift to accommodate our new frequency.

Dr. Carmen tracked her multiplication effect: "I started by healing my own fragmentation. Within a year, my team of 12 began integrating their whole selves. They influenced their teams. Three years later, our entire division (400 people) operated from new paradigms. The CEO asked me to lead the company-wide culture transformation. My personal healing is reshaping a Fortune 500 company."

This is the sacred mathematics of multiplication: Your liberation doesn't add to collective freedom—it multiplies it exponentially.

Transform your grand vision into daily liberation practices.

Liberation leadership isn't additional work—it's a lens for all work:

Morning Practice: Before opening email, set liberation intention: "How will I create more freedom today?" This primes your unconscious to seek liberation opportunities.

Meeting Alchemy: Before entering any meeting, ask: "How can I expand possibilities here?" Watch how this question transforms your participation. You'll interrupt limiting patterns, suggest innovative approaches, and make space for unheard voices.

Decision Filter: With every choice, consider liberation impact: "Does this create more freedom or more constriction?" Apply to hiring decisions, project approvals, schedule choices, and communication styles.

Email Liberation: Transform routine communications into freedom expansion. Instead of "Per my last email," try "Building on our conversation, here's an even better possibility..." Make every exchange create more spaciousness.

Presentation Revolution: Include liberation metrics in every presentation. Alongside ROI and KPIs, show DHI (Diversity & Healing Impact). Normalize measuring wholeness alongside profit.

Evening Reflection: Before bed, journal: "What freedom did I create today? What constriction did I transform?" Celebrate micro-liberations—they accumulate into macro-transformation.

Micro-liberation moments compound:

Using someone's correct pronouns = identity liberation

Amplifying a quiet voice in meetings = expression liberation

Questioning an outdated policy = systemic liberation

Taking lunch away from your desk = self-care liberation

Crediting ideas accurately = intellectual liberation

Dr. Ayana practiced daily liberation leadership: "I stopped seeing it as extra work and recognized it as the real work. Every interaction became an opportunity to create more freedom. Within six months, my team meetings transformed from obligation to innovation labs. People started saying, 'I've never felt so free to be creative at work.'"

Dedicate your leadership to collective liberation through ceremony.

Choose a significant date—birthday, new moon, ancestor day. Gather:

Photos or names of ancestors whose liberation work you continue

Images representing your future legacy

Candle for each generation (past, present, future)

Your Liberation Blueprint

Sacred objects representing your leadership

The Liberation Legacy Ceremony:

Create Sacred Space: Light incense, play music that moves your spirit, call in your highest self, and help ancestors.

Honor the Past: Light an ancestor candle. Speak: "I honor all who fought for the freedom I inherit. Your struggle was not in vain. I carry your torch forward with reverence and determination."

Claim the Present: Light your candle. Read your Liberation Blueprint aloud. Feel the words vibrate through your body, encoding themselves in your cells.

Bless the Future: Light a descendant candle. Write a letter to a future Black woman leader who will stand on your shoulders. Tell her what you're creating for her. Promise her that you'll heal. Share the wisdom you're preserving.

Sacred Vow: Stand with all candles burning. Speak:

"I lead not for power but for liberation.

I succeed not for self but for the sovereignty of all.

My legacy lives not in what I accumulate but in who I free.

I am the ancestor my descendants will thank.

I am the leader my ancestors prayed for.

I am liberation in motion.

And so it is."

Integration: Dance, sing, move your body. Let liberation flow through your entire being. Feel yourself as part of the great chain of liberation workers stretching through time.

Closing: Thank all beings present. Blow out candles, sending liberation energy to all directions. Keep your letter to future generations on your altar.

Your liberation legacy has already begun.

Every sovereign choice you've made has shifted the field. Every boundary set has created new possibilities. Every truth spoken has planted seeds in consciousness. You may not see all the fruits yet, but trust—gardens grow in seasons, not seconds.

Some will liberate because of your direct mentorship. Others will transform simply from witnessing your example. Still others will be influenced by people you influenced, liberation rippling through networks you'll never fully trace.

This is how we change the world—not through grand gestures alone but through daily choices to lead from liberation. Not through perfection but through practice. Not through arrival but through the journey.

You lead not because you've completed your healing but because your healing helps others heal. Your liberation legacy lives in every soul who breathes freer because you chose sovereignty.

Feel into the profound responsibility and profound gift of this moment. You stand at the intersection of all who came before and all who will come after. Your choices echo through generations. Your healing reverberates through time.

Rise, Liberation Leader. Your legacy is already writing itself through your very existence. Make it conscious. Make it powerful. Make it so liberating that future generations will speak your name with the same reverence you speak your ancestors'.

The collective liberation you seek begins with the sovereign leadership you embody.

Lead on. We're all rising with you.

11

Wealth as Spiritual Practice and Social Justice

Your money story was written before you could hold a pencil.

Let's excavate the colonial programming running your financial operating system. These stories, inherited like brown eyes or broad hips, shape every financial decision you make. Time to dig them up, examine them in light, and rewrite them in liberation's ink.

"Money doesn't grow on trees." The scarcity scripture, passed down from generations who knew lack as a constant companion. But what if money does grow on trees—the trees of your expertise, your innovation, your value? What if scarcity is the lie and abundance is the truth they didn't want you to know?

Decolonized rewrite: "Money flows to me as naturally as leaves grow on trees—through my gifts, my purpose, my divine assignment."

"Rich people are evil." The protective programming, meant to make poverty feel noble rather than imposed. But evil isn't about bank balance—it's about exploitation. Building ethical wealth that elevates the community isn't evil. It's evolution.

Decolonized rewrite: "Wealth in conscious hands creates healing. I build riches that enrich all beings."

"We're not those kinds of people." The class limitation lock keeps you in the assigned economic station. But who decided what kind of people you are? The same systems that profit from your poverty?

Decolonized rewrite: "We are exactly the kind of people who deserve abundance—we who have created wealth for others for centuries deserve to create it for ourselves."

"Good girls don't talk about money." The silent story is keeping you from negotiating, investing, and building. But silence about money serves only those who benefit from your ignorance.

Decolonized rewrite: "Sovereign women speak money fluently, creating prosperity through conscious conversation."

Take out your journal. Title a page "My Money Archaeological Dig."

What's your earliest money memory? Not the coins in birthday cards, but the moment money meant something. Maybe watching your mother count bills with worried eyes. Perhaps hearing parents argue about expenses. Or the moment you realized your family had less than others.

Map your family's money patterns:

How did grandmother relate to money? (Probably through lack and making do)

How did mother handle money? (Often through anxiety and overwork)

What money messages did you receive without words? (The tension when bills arrived, the relief on payday, the shame around hand-me-downs)

Track your spending/earning triggers:

What emotions arise when you pay bills?

How do you feel about receiving payment for your work?

What body sensations accompany financial decisions?

For Black women, money stories carry extra weight. We learn early that our labor is worth less, our expertise questioned more, our prosperity more threatening. We inherit stories of ancestors whose wages were stolen, whose businesses were burned, whose wealth was systematically destroyed through policy and violence.

Dr. Keisha discovered patterns: "I realized I always undercharged because I'd internalized that Black women's work was worth less. I'd literally encoded pay discrimination into my pricing. Once I saw it, I could heal it."

Somatic practice for releasing money trauma: Stand with feet hip-width apart. Breathe into your belly. Say aloud: "I release all inherited money trauma from my body." Shake vigorously for 60 seconds, imagining old stories flying off like water. Then stand still, breathe, and speak your new money truth: "I am worthy of abundant wealth. My prosperity heals generations."

Your decolonized money manifesto isn't just personal transformation—it's reparations for generations of economic violence.

Wealth building as a spiritual practice requires understanding money as energy.

The Sacred Wealth Wheel contains eight spokes, each one essential for sustainable prosperity:

Consciousness: Your wealth begins in your mind. Every morning, before checking bank balances, check your abundance consciousness. Are you operating from scarcity or sufficiency? Practice: Start each day writing ten things you're wealthy in—health, relationships, creativity. Train your consciousness to recognize existing abundance.

Reception: Your capacity to receive determines your wealth. Many Black women excel at giving but struggle with receiving—we've been programmed that our worth comes from depletion. Practice: This week, accept every compliment fully. Let someone buy you coffee. Receive support without immediately reciprocating. Build your reception muscle.

Creation: You are a wealth creator, not just an earner. Shift from trading time for money to creating value that multiplies. Practice: Identify three ways your expertise could generate passive income. What knowledge could become courses? What systems could become templates? Create wealth vehicles.

Circulation: Money must flow to grow. Hoarding from fear creates stagnation. Conscious circulation creates multiplication. Practice: Create a "Sacred Circulation" fund—10% of income that flows to Black women's businesses, liberation work, or community healing. Watch how giving consciously increases receiving.

Multiplication: Every dollar can become ten through conscious investment. But first, heal investment trauma from predatory lending, pyramid schemes, and financial abuse targeting our communities. Practice: Start with micro-investments. $25 monthly into index funds. $50 into Black-owned businesses. Learn through doing.

Protection: Protecting wealth is holy work when systems actively try to extract it from us. This isn't fear—it's wisdom. Practice: Get clear on insurance, estate planning, and asset protection. Hire Black women professionals when possible. Protection ensures your wealth serves generations.

Distribution: How wealth flows through you determines its sacred nature. Random giving dissipates power; strategic distribution multiplies impact. Practice: Create giving strategies aligned with your liberation blueprint. Fund what you want to see grow.

Evolution: Your wealth consciousness must evolve continuously. What got you to six figures won't get you to seven. Practice: Quarterly wealth consciousness check-ins. Where are you still operating from old stories? What new elevation is required?

Daily Wealth Practice (10 minutes):

Morning: "Abundance Activation"—speak gratitude for existing wealth

Midday: "Conscious Money Movement"—bless every transaction

Evening: "Prosperity Visioning"—imagine your wealth serving liberation

Example practice from Dr. Amara: "I bless every dollar that flows to and through me. I track my money with love, not fear. I celebrate others' wealth, knowing abundance is infinite. Before major purchases, I ask: Does this align with my values? Will this create more freedom? I've turned budgeting into a spiritual practice."

Money becomes medicine when infused with consciousness. Your wealth practice heals you, your lineage, and the collective.

Your Liberation Wealth Plan bridges the spiritual and practical.

Start with visioning: How will wealth serve your liberation legacy? Perhaps funding scholarships for Black girls in STEM. Maybe purchasing land to create healing centers. Or building businesses that employ formerly incarcerated women. Get specific about wealth as tool for collective freedom.

Define your three numbers:

Freedom Number: The amount needed for personal sovereignty—all bills paid, emergency fund full, some pleasures funded. Often lower than we think. Calculate: essential expenses × 12 + emergency fund (6 months expenses) + joy fund (10% of annual expenses). This number creates baseline freedom.

Legacy Number: The amount needed to fund your liberation blueprint. If your vision includes mentoring 100 women, calculate program costs. If it's creating healing centers, research real estate. This number makes vision tangible.

Liberation Number: The amount that creates systematic change. Endowing scholarships in perpetuity. Funding reparations initiatives. Creating investment funds for Black women entrepreneurs. This number transforms systems.

Strategies for each stage:

Reaching Freedom Number:

Negotiate current salary (Black women leave $1 million on the table through under-negotiation)

Create additional revenue streams aligned with expertise

Automate savings (pay yourself first, ancestors insisted)

Reduce expenses that don't align with values

Achieving Legacy Number:

Scale expertise through programs, not just hours

Build an investment portfolio with conscious choices

Create intellectual property that generates passive income

Collaborate with aligned souls for bigger impact

Manifesting Liberation Number:

Build businesses that solve systemic problems

Create investment vehicles for collective wealth

Partner with other sovereign leaders for exponential impact

Think generations, not just years

Common challenges and solutions:

Family money dynamics: "Now that you have money..." Set boundaries early, create giving budgets, and teach financial literacy

Survivor guilt: Remember, your success creates possibility templates. Guilt serves no one; modeling prosperity serves many

Visibility fears: Safety strategies while building wealth. Privacy tools, security measures, trusted advisors

Dr. Sasha navigated beautifully: "I created three pots: personal freedom, family support, and community liberation. Clear boundaries prevented resentment. My wealth serves all of us, but strategically."

Tax strategies as resistance:

Legal tax reduction isn't cheating—it's keeping resources for liberation work

Hire Black women CPAs who understand both strategy and mission

See tax planning as ensuring more money serves the community, not just the government

Use tax savings for reparative giving

Estate planning as ancestor honoring:

Create trusts that protect and direct wealth

Include charitable giving that continues your liberation work

Write ethical wills sharing wisdom alongside wealth

Ensure your assets strengthen rather than divide the family

Your Liberation Wealth Plan isn't just personal financial planning—it's strategic resource accumulation for collective freedom.

Reframe personal wealth building as active reparations.

The mathematics of theft are staggering. Calculate:

246 years of stolen labor during slavery: $5-10 trillion in today's dollars

Destroyed Black Wall Streets: Over 35 prosperous Black communities burned

Redlining theft: $212,000 average loss per Black family through housing discrimination

Pay gap extraction: $946,120 lost over career for average Black woman

This isn't about guilt—it's about clarity. Your wealth building isn't selfish. It's corrective. Every dollar you accumulate helps balance cosmic scales tipped by centuries of theft.

Dr. Nia calculated her family's specific losses: "Great-grandmother's stolen wages, grandfather's burned business, parents' redlining losses—total: $3.2 million. My wealth goal? $3.2 million. I'm not building wealth. I'm reclaiming it."

Reparative wealth-building strategies:

Buy back Black land (over 90% lost since 1910)

Invest in Black businesses (only 2% of venture capital goes to Black founders)

Create employment specifically for Black women

Fund liberation work—movements, healers, artists, revolutionaries

The Reparations Mathematics:

Calculate what was stolen from your lineage (even estimates heal)

Set wealth goals that account for this theft

Create giving strategies that repair collective wounds

Track how your wealth-building heals historical harm

Example: Dr. Keyana bought the block where her great-grandmother's house was stolen through eminent domain. She's creating affordable housing for Black elders. "My wealth is literally reclaiming what was taken. That's reparations in action."

Remember: Your wealth doesn't just benefit you. It begins healing centuries of economic violence. Every investment property you buy could have been owned by ancestors without discrimination. Every business you build could have been your great-grandmother's without Jim Crow. You're not starting from zero—you're continuing an interrupted legacy.

Sacred Wealth Practices infuse money with spiritual power.

Morning Abundance Ritual (5 minutes):

Light green candle (color of growth and money)

Place hands on wallet/purse

Speak: "I am a prosperous child of a prosperous universe"

Visualize money flowing to you from all directions

Thank money for its service to your liberation

New Moon Wealth Seeding (monthly):

Write financial intentions for the lunar cycle

Be specific: "I attract three new clients at my full rate"

Create a vision board for that month's wealth goals

Plant literal seeds while speaking intentions

Water seeds daily while affirming abundance

Full Moon Money Clearing (monthly):

Review all accounts under full moonlight

Release scarcity beliefs: write and burn them

Cleanse wallet/purse with sage or incense

Place citrine (abundance stone) in wallet

Dance to celebrate existing wealth

Weekly Money Dates:

Schedule sacred time with your finances

Light candles, play beautiful music

Review with love, not fear

Celebrate every penny earned and saved

Plan upcoming wealth moves with joy

Advanced Practices:

Money Reiki: Send healing energy to bank accounts

Ancestor Money Burning: Honor lineage while calling in abundance

Collective Wealth Ceremonies: Gather with other sovereign women for group abundance rituals

Create your Sacred Wealth Altar:

Green cloth as base (growth and money)

Coins from birth year (personal prosperity)

Photo of prosperous ancestor or role model

Citrine, pyrite, or green aventurine crystals

Fresh flowers (life and growth)

Your Liberation Wealth Plan

Daily practice: Spend 2 minutes at the altar speaking gratitude and intentions.

When wealth building becomes a spiritual practice, money transforms from master to medicine.

Individual wealth building connects to collective prosperity through conscious community.

The "Each One Teach One" wealth principle means your financial literacy becomes community liberation. But this isn't the old model of one queen and many servants. This is circular economics—everyone rises.

Creating Wealth Circles:

Selecting Aligned Souls (5-7 women):

Similar values, different expertise

Commitment to collective rise

Mix of wealth levels for mutual learning

Racial consciousness (all Black or consciously mixed)

Establishing Agreements:

Confidentiality about specific numbers

Commitment to regular meetings

No judgment about current wealth levels

Celebration of all gains

Support through losses

Sample Meeting Structure (2 hours monthly):

Opening ritual (5 min)

Wins and challenges round (30 min)

Financial education segment (30 min)

Strategy session for one member (30 min)

Collective visioning (20 min)

Closing ritual (5 min)

Collective Investment Strategies:

Group investment club ($50-500/month each)

Collective property purchases

Group funding for members' businesses

Shared resources (accountants, attorneys, advisors)

Dr. Michelle's wealth circle transformed five women's finances: "We started with a combined net worth of negative $50,000. Three years later, we're at $2.8 million collective net worth. We learned together, invested together, rose together."

Address the isolation many feel about money. Shame thrives in shadows but dies in sharing. Creating a conscious wealth community breaks the spell of secrecy that keeps us small.

You deserve wealth. You deserve ease. You deserve to build prosperity without apology. Your wealth is medicine this world desperately needs.

Close this chapter by creating a ceremony for your wealth commitment.

Gather:

Your decolonized money manifesto

Your Liberation Wealth Plan

Green candle

Bowl of water

Coins

The Wealth Liberation Ceremony:

Light a candle, calling in abundance ancestors

Read the manifesto aloud with power

State your three numbers clearly

Drop coins in water, one for each wealth goal

Speak: "I commit to building wealth as spiritual practice and social justice. My prosperity serves liberation. My abundance heals generations. I am reparations in motion."

Drink the water, integrating commitment

Dance, celebrating the wealthy woman you're becoming

Your wealth is not just personal gain—it's generational healing, systemic disruption, and collective liberation. Every dollar you earn with consciousness, invest with wisdom, and circulate with love becomes medicine for wounds centuries deep.

Build wealth like your ancestors' wildest dreams depend on it. Because they do.

Rise, wealthy one. Your prosperity is holy. Your abundance is healing. Your wealth is the justice this world desperately needs.

12

Crowning the Sovereign Queen Within

You've gathered crown jewels on this journey, each one hard-won and irreplaceable.

The Ruby of Remembering (Chapter 1): The blood-red recognition that your fragmentation wasn't failure but a survival strategy whose time had passed. This jewel catches light whenever impostor syndrome tries to resurface, reminding you that you belong everywhere you choose to be.

The Sapphire of Liberation (Chapter 2): Deep blue as the night sky that holds all stars, this gem freed you from ancestral contracts that no longer served. You wear it as a reminder that you can honor your lineage while writing new rules.

The Emerald of Integration (Chapter 3): Green as growth itself, this jewel merged your spiritual wisdom with professional power. No more choosing between success and soul—this gem proves they're dance partners, not competitors.

The Diamond of Boundaries (Chapter 4): Clear, strong, multifaceted—your boundaries now refract light rather than blocking it. This jewel reminds you that protecting your energy multiplies rather than diminishes your impact.

The Amethyst of Alchemy (Chapter 5): Purple as royal robes, this gem transformed your wounds into wisdom. Every scar became a star map guiding others through similar terrain.

The Pearl of Voice (Chapter 6): Formed through pressure into luminous beauty, your voice now carries the authority of authentic expression. This jewel glows whenever you speak your truth.

The Opal of Reflection (Chapter 7): Showing different colors from different angles, this gem taught you that others' reactions mirror their readiness, not your worth. You wear it as protection against taking things personally.

The Obsidian of Resilience (Chapter 8): Black volcanic glass forged in fire, this jewel showed you how to dance with resistance rather than fight it. Strong enough to cut through obstacles, smooth enough to flow around them.

The Rose Quartz of Connection (Chapter 9): Soft pink as dawn, this gem dissolved the myth of solo success. Your constellation of support now holds you as you hold others.

The Citrine of Legacy (Chapter 10): Golden as generational wealth, this jewel transformed personal success into collective liberation. Every achievement now serves someone beyond yourself.

The Gold of Prosperity (Chapter 11): Pure, valuable, malleable—your relationship with wealth transformed from guilty secret to sacred tool. This metal now funds freedom, not just lifestyle.

Rate your embodiment of each jewel from 1-10. Not for judgment but for celebration and clarity. Where you score 8-10, celebrate the integration. Where you score 4-6, celebrate the growth edge. Where you score 1-3, celebrate the clarity of what wants attention next.

These aren't external achievements but internal alchemical shifts that can never be taken away. You are permanently jeweled.

Sovereignty requires daily practice, like tending a sacred garden.

Your Sovereignty Embodiment Practice:

Morning Coronation (5 minutes):

Stand before your mirror. Place your hand on your crown. Speak: "I am sovereign. I am whole. I am enough. I lead from my throne today." Feel the crown of energy activate. Carry this feeling into your day.

Boundary Blessing (throughout day):

Before entering any space—physical or virtual—pause. Touch your solar plexus. Choose consciously: "I enter this space sovereign. I engage from choice, not obligation." Feel your energetic boundaries activate like golden armor.

Voice Activation (before speaking):

Touch your throat lightly. Breathe into your power center. Ask: "What wants to be spoken through me?" Let your voice carry the full spectrum of your truth. Notice when you're about to modulate and choose authenticity instead.

Prosperity Practice (with every transaction):

As money flows to or from you, pause. Bless the exchange: "This money serves liberation." Feel yourself as a channel for conscious wealth circulation. Track the feeling of abundance versus scarcity.

Evening Integration (10 minutes):

Journal three sovereignty moments from your day. Where did you choose from your throne? What queenly decisions did you make? How did your sovereignty serve others? Celebrate every conscious choice.

Weekly Sovereignty Sabbath:

Choose one day weekly for deep sovereignty renewal. Longer morning practice. Sacred bathing. Reviewing your journey. Planning your queenly week. Non-negotiable time for the queen to restore.

Monthly Crown Council:

Gather your support constellation. Share sovereignty challenges and victories. Practice witnessing each other's majesty. Create accountability for continued embodiment. Celebrate collective queendom.

Quarterly Coronation Renewal:

Every season, renew your vows to yourself. Review your sovereignty practices. Adjust what's not serving. Amplify what's working. Re-crown yourself with an evolved understanding.

Annual Legacy Review:

Each year, assess your liberation legacy. What freedom have you created? Who has risen because you rose? How has your sovereignty served collective liberation? Plan your next year of queenly impact.

The non-negotiable nature of practice: Sovereignty isn't an achievement but a practice. Like physical fitness, it requires consistent cultivation. Not perfection—practice. Your queendom depends on these daily choices.

Translate sovereign queendom into every sphere of your life.

In Professional Spaces:

Lead meetings from your energetic center, not your strategic mind alone. Let your presence shift the field before you speak. Make decisions that honor your whole knowing. Model integration through your very being. Create policies that reflect sovereignty principles. Mentor from queen to emerging queen.

In Relationships:

Maintain boundaries while deepening intimacy—sovereignty creates space for true connection. Love from fullness, not neediness. Give from overflow, not depletion. Receive as queenly right, not guilty pleasure. Model what mutual sovereignty looks like.

In Community:

Use your power for collective liberation always. Create platforms for other voices. Share resources strategically. Build new tables rather than only seeking seats. Lead movements from service, not ego. Remember: a true queen creates more queens.

In the Financial Realm:

Make money moves from abundance consciousness. Invest in alignment with values. Build wealth that serves liberation. Model conscious prosperity. Teach financial sovereignty. Create economic ecosystems that nurture collective rise.

In Spiritual Practice:

Generate from within rather than seeking external validation. Trust your direct connection to the divine source. Create practices that honor your unique path. Integration rather than separation of the spiritual and material. Your whole life becomes spiritual practice.

Create your Sovereignty Signatures—specific ways you'll lead differently:

"I enter all rooms grounded in my worth."

"I speak first in meetings, modeling voiced leadership."

"I collaborate rather than compete with other queens."

"I rest as a revolutionary act."

"I build wealth without apology."

Every sphere of your life becomes a realm in your queendom. You don't have sovereignty—you are sovereignty.

Your individual sovereignty creates exponential collective transformation.

The mathematics are staggering: If just 1,000 readers fully embody sovereignty, and each impacts 10 others directly, that's 10,000 sovereign beings in the first wave. When those 10,000 influence their circles, we reach 100,000. By the third degree of separation, one million Black women lead fromsovereignty.

But this underestimates the morphic field principle. As more Black women embody sovereignty, the energetic template shifts. What was once difficult becomes natural. What required courage becomes common. The field itself reorganizes to support sovereignty rather than resist it.

Visualize it: Golden threads connecting every sovereign Black woman leader, creating an energetic grid across continents. Each time you choose sovereignty, the grid strengthens. Each boundary set sends signals to sisters globally. Each truth spoken reverberates through the web. You're not just changing yourself—you're uploading new templates to collective consciousness.

Your Sovereignty Multiplication Commitment:

"I mentor three emerging queens yearly."

"I create content that activates sovereignty in others."

"I model sovereign leadership publicly."

"I hire and promote other sovereign women."

"I fund sovereignty activation programs."

Dr. Carmen tracked her multiplication: "In five years of sovereign leadership, I've directly mentored 50 Black women into senior positions. They've each influenced their teams. Conservatively, my sovereignty has impacted 5,000 careers. This is how we change everything—one queen creating more queens."

Your sovereignty isn't complete until all Black women are free to claim theirs. We crown ourselves together or not at all.

Create your personal coronation ceremony as initiation into a lifelong queendom.

Choose your date carefully—new moon for new beginnings, full moon for fullness, birthday for rebirth, or any date that carries personal significance. This isn't graduation—it's initiation.

Preparation:

Choose location: home altar, natural setting, or sacred space

Invite witnesses: sister circle, mentors, or conduct solo

Gather elements: crown (can be flowers, jewelry, or energetic), candle for each chapter, your journey journal, mirror, ceremonial clothing

Opening Sacred Space:

Light incense or sage. Call in directions, ancestors, and guides. Play music that moves your soul. Create a circle of protection and celebration.

Reflection Journey:

Light a candle for each chapter, speaking aloud your transformation:

"With this flame, I honor the remembering that called me home..."

"With this light, I celebrate breaking ancestral contracts..."

Continue through all twelve, feeling the journey in your body.

Releasing the Old:

Write on paper what you release: impostor syndrome, fragmentation, unworthiness, playing small. Burn safely, speaking: "I release all that no longer serves my sovereignty. I am free."

Declaration of Sovereignty:

Stand before the mirror. Look into your own eyes. Speak your vows:

"I crown myself Sovereign Queen of my own life.

I claim my throne as birthright, not achievement.

I lead with integrated power and conscious love.

I speak truth with grace and strategy.

I build wealth as justice and spiritual practice.

I create legacy through liberation.

I am whole. I am enough. I am sovereign.

And so it is."

The Crowning:

Place crown on your head (physical or energetic). Feel the weight and honor of sovereignty. Let tears come if they come. Let laughter emerge if it emerges. This is your moment.

Integration Celebration:

Dance! Move your sovereign body. Let your queenly energy flow through every cell. Feel yourself as a crowned leader, sacred vessel, liberation worker, ancestor's dream.

Closing:

Thank all beings present. Commit to daily sovereignty practice. Share the feast with others. Journal your experience. Sleep in your crown (literally or energetically).

This coronation marks not your arrival but your conscious beginning as sovereign queen. The real work starts now.

This ending is actually a commencement.

Letter from your future self, five years hence:

"Beloved Queen,

I write to you from a life you're still creating. Your sovereignty has bloomed beyond what you can currently imagine. The boundaries you're setting become the foundation for an empire of impact. The voice you're freeing becomes a clarion call for thousands. The wealth you're building funds movements. The legacy you're creating ripples through generations.

But more than external achievement, you've found something precious: sustainable joy. The exhaustion that once defined you is a memory. The fragmentation healed so completely that you struggle to remember that split feeling. You lead from such integrated wholeness that others forget there's any other way.

Keep going. Every sovereignty practice matters. Every boundary strengthens our collective field. Every truth spoken creates more space for truth. You're not just changing your life—you're changing the template for Black women's leadership globally.

With infinite love and crown-to-crown recognition,

Your Future Sovereign Self"

Your Sovereignty Success Plan for the next 90 days:

- Three practices to embody daily (choose from this chapter)
- Three old patterns to release (be specific)
- Three legacy actions to take (start small, but start)

Month 1: Internal sovereignty strengthening

Month 2: External sovereignty expression

Month 3: Collective sovereignty activation

Track daily: "How did I choose from my throne today?"

Track weekly: "What shifted because of my sovereignty?"

Track monthly: "How is my queendom expanding?"

Resources for continued journey:

Create an accountability partnership with another sovereign queen

Join or create a Crown Council for ongoing support

Book quarterly sovereignty retreats (even one day)

Develop your own sovereignty teaching to share

Document your journey for the queens coming behind you

Sovereignty isn't a destination but a practice. You haven't arrived—you've consciously begun.

Final Blessing:

You came seeking a crown and discovered it was woven into your DNA. You thought sovereignty was something to achieve and learned it was something to remember. You believed you needed permission and realized you were the permission others were waiting for.

Every page you've read has been an activation. Every practice you've done has been renovation. Every resistance you've faced has been initiation. You are not the same woman who opened this book. You couldn't be. The old templates have been overwritten. The new patterns are encoded. The sovereignty virus is uploaded—in the best way.

Now you know: The exhausted woman was never weak—she was carrying too much that wasn't hers. The fragmented woman was never broken—she was strategic in her survival. The silenced woman was never voiceless—she was waiting for a safe space to speak. That woman? She's integrated now. Whole. Sovereign. Free.

But sovereignty in isolation serves no one. Your crown means nothing if others remain uncrowned. Your throne matters only as inspiration for others to claim theirs. Your liberation stays incomplete until we all taste freedom.

So rise, Sovereign Queen. Rise and create a world where Black women lead from wholeness. Rise and model what integrated power looks like. Rise and build tables where everyone feasts. Rise and speak truths that transform systems. Rise and build wealth that heals wounds. Rise and crown others as you've been crowned.

You are the sovereign queen your ancestors prayed for. You are the leader your descendants need. You are the transformation this world is desperate to see. Your time is now. Your throne awaits. Your queendom begins with your next breath.

Place your hand on your crown one last time. Feel the energy there—not new but newly acknowledged. Speak your name preceded by "Queen." Let it settle into your bones. Let it reprogram your cells. Let it be the truth you never again question.

The Goddess Gateway has been crossed. The threshold is behind you. What lies ahead is the queendom you're building with every sovereign choice.

Lead on, Goddess Queen. We're all rising with you.

13

APPENDIX A

The Goddess Gateway Practice Compendium

A Quick Reference Guide to Sovereign Embodiment

ESSENTIAL PRACTICES: The Foundation of Your Sovereignty

CHAPTER 1: The Remembering Calls You Home

Practice: The Recognition & Reclamation Writing

What: Identify 3 ways you fragment yourself + 3 small integration actions for the week.

When: Upon starting the book, and whenever you feel disconnected.

How: Write quickly without judgment. Pair each fragmentation with one tangible, gentle act of reclamation.

Affirmation: "I choose wholeness. My spiritual wisdom enhances my professional power."

CHAPTER 2: Breaking the Ancestral Silence Contract

Practice: Speaking the Unspoken Names

What: A verbal ritual to reclaim the true titles of your ancestors' hidden gifts.

When: During quiet, sacred space (with a candle/ancestral object).

How: Speak aloud: "My grandmother, [Name], was a [Seer/Healer/Prophet], not just 'intuitive.'" Replace minimizing language with full truth.
Affirmation: "I nullify the silence contract. My voice carries ancestral truth."

CHAPTER 3: The Alchemy of Integration

Practice: The Integration Initiation & Intention
What: A somatic ritual to fuse your spiritual and professional selves.
When: When feeling fragmented or before a challenging day.
How: Hold objects representing your spiritual self (left hand) and professional self (right hand). Bring them together at your heart. Write one specific Integration Intention for the week.
Affirmation: "I am one woman, indivisible. My spirituality informs my strategy."

CHAPTER 4: The Sacred Art of Divine Boundaries

Practice: The 21-Day Boundary Temple Construction
What: A three-week structured program to build robust energetic boundaries.
When: When feeling drained or overwhelmed by others' demands.
How: Week 1: Identify 3 energy leaks; practice one small "no" daily. Week 2: Set 3 non-negotiable boundaries. Week 3: Implement boundaries in challenging relationships.
Affirmation: "My no is a sacred yes to my purpose."

CHAPTER 5: Alchemy of the Wounded Healer

Practice: Creating Your Medicine Bundle & Mission Statement
What: Physically gather objects representing your journey from wound to wisdom.
When: After identifying a core wound that has transformed.

How: Arrange objects consciously. Speak to each: Thank you for the medicine you helped me make. Create your Healer-Leader Mission Statement.

Affirmation: "My wounds are the raw material for my unique medicine."

CHAPTER 6: Reclaiming Your Throne Room Voice

Practice: The 13-Day Voice Restoration Journey

What: A progressive journey to reclaim the full spectrum of your authentic voice.

When: When you notice silencing yourself or modulating to please others.

How: Days 1-3: Throat chakra healing. Days 4-6: Reclaim ancestral voices. Days 7-9: Practice full vocal spectrum. Days 10-12: Strategic implementation. Day 13: Voice Vow ceremony.

Affirmation: "My voice is sacred medicine. I speak my truth with power and grace."

CHAPTER 7: The Mirror Work of Authentic Authority

Practice: The Discernment Matrix

What: A filter for evaluating feedback/resistance.

When: Whenever you receive challenging feedback or face pushback.

How: Ask: 1. Source 2. Content 3. Pattern 4. Energy 5. Outcome. Assess if feedback makes you more powerful or smaller.

Affirmation: "I am a sacred mirror. I welcome reflections that reveal where I must grow."

ADVANCED PRACTICES: For Deepened Embodiment & Legacy

CHAPTER 8: Dancing with Resistance and Revelation

Practice: The Sovereign Alkaline Protocol

What: A daily practice to transform resistance into fuel for your power.

When: Daily practice, with special attention before challenging situations.

How: Morning: Ground barefoot, breathe golden light. Interaction: Touch power talisman before challenges. Evening: Shake body, journal insights. Weekly: Deep clearing.

Affirmation: "I am an alchemist of resistance. Every challenge is intelligence."

CHAPTER 9: Building Your Sacred Support Constellation

Practice: The Reciprocity Reset Process

What: A systematic approach to rebalance your relationships.

When: Quarterly or when relationships feel draining.

How: Step 1: Audit relationships. Step 2: Identify imbalances. Step 3: Have conversations. Step 4: Create agreements. Step 5: Reassess quarterly.

Affirmation: "I give and receive in balanced, joyful reciprocity."

CHAPTER 10: The Leadership Legacy of Liberation

Practice: The Liberation Blueprint & Ceremony

What: Create a comprehensive vision for your liberatory legacy.

When: When ready to articulate your long-term impact.

How: Define Vision 2050, Mission, Values, Strategies, Metrics, Timeline. Ceremony: Light candles for past/present/future. Read Blueprint aloud. Speak Liberation Vow.

Affirmation: "I lead not for power, but for liberation. I am the ancestor my descendants will thank."

CHAPTER 11: Wealth as Spiritual Practice and Social Justice

Practice: The Sacred Wealth Wheel & Liberation Wealth Plan

What: An integrated approach to building wealth that serves liberation.

When: Monthly wealth planning and daily consciousness practice.

How: Tend to 8 spokes: Consciousness, Reception, Creation, Circulation, Multiplication, Protection, Distribution, Evolution. Define 3 Numbers: Freedom, Legacy, Liberation.

Affirmation: "My prosperity is holy. Every dollar I steward is a reclamation of stolen legacy."

CHAPTER 12: Crowning the Sovereign Queen Within

Practice: Sovereignty Embodiment Practice & Personal Coronation

What: Daily practices culminating in a ceremonial self-crowning.

When: Daily embodiment practice, with coronation ceremony when ready.

How: Daily: Morning coronation, boundary blessing, evening integration. Weekly Sabbath. Coronation: Prepare space, reflect, release, declare, crown, integrate.

Affirmation: "I crown myself Sovereign Goddess. My throne is my birthright, my legacy is liberation."

QUICK-REFERENCE TABLE: Practice by Challenge

When You Feel Fragmented, Inauthentic:

Ch. 1: Recognition Writing; Ch. 3: Integration Initiation

When You Feel Voiceless, Silenced:

Ch. 2: Speaking Unspoken Names; Ch. 6: 13-Day Voice Journey

When You Feel Drained, Depleted:

Ch. 4: 21-Day Boundary Temple; Ch. 9: Reciprocity Reset

When Triggered by Feedback/Pushback:

Ch. 7: Discernment Matrix; Ch. 8: Alkaline Protocol

When Stuck in Past Wounds:

Ch. 5: Medicine Bundle; Ch. 10: Lineage Healing Protocol

When Unclear on Purpose/Legacy:

Ch. 10: Liberation Blueprint; Ch. 12: Sovereignty Practice

When Anxious About Money/Wealth:

Ch. 11: Wealth Wheel; Liberation Wealth Plan

When Needing Ceremonial Commitment:

Ch. 12: Personal Coronation; Ch. 10: Liberation Ceremony

When Feeling Isolated, Unsupported:

Ch. 9: Constellation Mapping; Reciprocity Reset

A Final Note:

These practices are not linear milestones but a cyclical toolkit. Return to them as needed. Sovereignty is a practice, not a perfection. Your consistent return to these rituals is the surest path to embodied, unshakable power.

May this compendium serve as a faithful companion on your endless journey of becoming.

About the Author

Dr. Camille Valentine's research delves into how professional BIPOCs can unmask and conquer Impostor Syndrome, relieve stress to enhance performance, and avoid burnout while building leadership confidence.

Specializing in change management and personal development, Dr. Valentine provides transformational emotional support that helps clients celebrate their successes, recognize their worth, and navigate the challenges of tokenism, systemic racism, and microaggressions rooted in Organizationally Induced Intrapersonal Trauma (O.I.I.T.).

Her work underscores the profound connection between impostor syndrome and chronic workplace stress, revealing how these dynamics erode job satisfaction, reduce engagement, and lead to burnout. For BIPOC professionals, these issues are often compounded by racial identity struggles and toxic work environments.

Dr. Valentine emphasizes that even the strongest individuals can face impostor syndrome without proper affirmation, support, and inclusive workplace cultures.

In response, Dr. Valentine created support groups designed to restore self-esteem, focus, and resilience, empowering individuals to unlock their unlimited potential.

With over two decades of experience as a Master Trainer in Alternative Dispute Resolution and an Intuitive Problem Solver, she drives transformative change at both individual and systemic levels.

Her evidence-based, human-centered approach fosters engagement, minimizes conflict, and builds authentic self-recognition and empowerment, enhancing leadership effectiveness and workplace culture. These efforts contribute directly to increased innovation, sustainability, and profitability.

As a dynamic speaker, Dr. Valentine captivates audiences with her strategies for overcoming Impostor Syndrome and creating legacies that extend beyond careers. CEOs, HR directors, and other leaders rely on her expertise to improve well-being and drive sustainable success.

Whether through speaking, coaching, or consulting, Dr. Valentine serves as a beacon of resilience and hope, guiding individuals and organizations toward lasting, positive change.

Connect with Dr. Valentine

Impostor Syndrome Speaker | Coach | Consultant | Author

Email: dr.camille@valentinecc.com

Phone: (559) 455-3080 (text ok)

LinkedIn: linkedin.com/in/drcamillevalentine

YouTube: youtube.com/@dr.camillevalentine

Acknowledgements

To the women who mothered me in every season—

My circle of surrogate moms whose guidance, protection, and unconditional love filled the spaces life tried to hollow out.

Thank you for holding me, shaping me, and reminding me who I am when the world demanded I forget.

To the strong and supportive women in my family, whose resilience is the foundation I stand on.

Your strength is my inheritance,
and your love is my home.

And to my Goddess Queen Besties—
my sovereign sisters for life—

Thank you for being my mirrors, my witnesses, and my sacred council of truth-tellers.

You are the ones who prayed for me, laughed with me, challenged me, and elevated me. This book carries your fingerprints,
your encouragement, and your belief in my becoming.

With Love Always, Camille

www.ingramcontent.com/pod-product-compliance
Lightning Source LLC
Chambersburg PA
CBHW030527080526
44586CB00011B/348